Extra Virgin Olive Oil

Advance Praise for *Extra Virgin Olive Oil*

"David Neuman knows as much about olive oil, both divine and disgusting, as anyone I've ever met—and cares more about leading consumers to the good stuff than anyone else I know. *Extra Virgin Olive Oil: The Truth in Your Kitchen*, based on his decades of experience in the olive oil trade, is essential reading for anyone who wants to find their way to great oil, and steer clear of the fraudulent junk so often sold as "extra virgin." As a trained taster and judge at international olive oil contests, he has a connoisseur's palate and has dined and walked the groves of many of the world's top producers. Yet, as a former executive in the mass market olive oil trade, he's also an authority on how oils are bought, sold, and distributed in supermarkets and food service. There is no better guide to the entire olive oil landscape and all of its secrets, both dark and luminous, than David Neuman. The only thing David cares more about than oil is people. He has made it his personal mission to awaken all consumers, so widely abused by Big Oil, to the unique flavors, aromas, and nutritional gifts of quality olive oil—and to steer clear of fake extra virgins and downright floozies that fill the store shelves. *Extra Virgin Olive Oil: The Truth in Your Kitchen* is the fruit of his decades of experience running oil companies, touring mills, training his palate at oil schools, judging international competitions, and generally immersing himself in this strange, wonderful world. This is your expert guide to finding quality oil. Buy this book."

—Tom Mueller,
New York Times best-selling author of *Extra Virginity*

"The health benefits of olive oil are found only in extra virgin, but knowing if your olive oil is extra virgin can be bewildering. Current labeling both domestically and internationally will not guarantee that the oil is extra virgin. David Neuman brings years of knowledge and experience and a healthy obsession with extra virgin olive oil that will help guide the consumer so they will purchase extra virgin olive oil. *Extra Virgin Olive Oil: The Truth in Your Kitchen* will go a long way to educating everyone on how to best ensure that you are buying extra virgin olive oil."

—Mary M. Flynn, PhD, RD, LDN,
associate professor of medicine and research dietitian
at The Miriam Hospital and Brown University.

"David Neuman is a man on a crusade to bring high-quality extra virgin olive oil to consumers with his EVOO guy truck and *Extra Virgin Olive Oil: The Truth in Your Kitchen*. In his truck, David guides consumers to recognize the sensory qualities of what true extra virgin olive oil should taste like. There is no substitute for tasting and using this guide; consumers will improve and gain confidence in their tasting abilities. Armed with this skill, consumers will become more discriminating: The unexamined olive oil is not worth consuming."

—Sue Langstaff,
co-author of *Olive Oil Sensory Science*, leader
of an accredited olive oil sensory taste panel,
instructor of "Sensory Evaluation Certificate
Course" at the UC-Davis Olive Center

"No one knows quality in olive oil and better able to teach how to choose it than David Neuman. The many health benefits of Mediterranean nutrition are only possible when using an olive oil high in its anti-inflammatory, life-giving antioxidants. David's book provides the consumer, physician, nutritionist, and health practitioner with an easy-to-read guide to choosing, storing, and tasting the essential ingredient of the Mediterranean diet: olive oil. After my patients, students, friends, and conference attendees hear about the health-promoting benefits of the Mediterranean diet, the next thing they want to know is, how do I choose a good, quality olive oil? David has made my job a lot easier by writing, *Extra Virgin Olive Oil: The Truth in Your Kitchen* which is the guide to becoming a master at-home taster. David taught me that the only way to really know your olive oil is to taste it, and *Extra Virgin Olive Oil: The Truth in Your Kitchen* is the field guide to a world of experience and sensitivity to quality."

—Artemis D Morris, ND, MS, L.Ac (Dipl. NCCAOM),
author of *The Anti-Inflammatory Diet for Dummies*
and physician specializing in Mediterranean nutrition

"I always say that if you cut my veins, you'll find olive oil. In the world, there are only a few other people I feel the same can be said about, and David Neuman is one of them. Though he did not grow up in a land with olive oil as the main source of fat and nutrition, David's passion for olive oil, from soil to bottle, is palpable—and because of this, his book is going to shine a light on the most precious and important aspect of the Mediterranean diet. As a chef who's life, career, and cuisine revolves around olive oil, I can honestly say that no one is more qualified to write *Extra Virgin Olive Oil: The Truth in Your Kitchen* than David Neuman."

—**Maria Loi,**
chef, author, restauranter, PBS TV chef,
EVOO brand owner Loi Estiatorio

"How does the EVOO connection reach an American from Washington DC? Where does that boundless passion flow from when it comes to a product so foreign to his culture? If it is thankfully becoming more and more familiar to an average American consumer, it's not because of the public institutions nor the most earnest olive growers, but by genuine pioneers like David, who have raised the quality banner and hurled it to spread the unrivalled benefits of EVOO, either among the main retailer's procurement managers or driving his truck along the countryside byroads. All my respect and admiration to a guy (indeed an *EVOOGuy*, as he calls himself) who has captured, as very few do, the magic of this millenary product and who works relentlessly to awaken Americans' curiosity, which currently, is at the mercy of dull and anodyne (if not often questionable) olive oils."

—**Jose Antonio Peche Marin Lazaro,**
general manager, *Casas de Hualdo* EVOO brand, Toledo, Spain

"I first met David in Chicago at an event show back in 2012. He was leading Lucini at that time and paving the way here in America for all of us in the olive oil industry. I was in the very early stages of distributing my family's olive oil direct from Greece, and David was someone I really admired in the business. I was surprised how approachable he was when I walked to his booth to introduce myself. David dropped everything he was doing, pulled me aside, and asked about my vision for my brand. I explained, and he responded with valuable advice. Advice that I desperately needed at the time. He didn't need to help me, but he chose to. That is David—willing to do whatever is needed to help expand quality-produced olive oil to consumers. *Extra Virgin Olive Oil: The Truth in Your Kitchen* is needed, and there is no one better in the world to write it. Thank you, David for standing up for me, and keep moving us all forward."

—Dimitri Kallianis,
founder, Lonely Olive Tree Organics

"David's passion for food, particularly his love of the Mediterranean Diet and specifically his expertise in olive oil, resonates throughout this book, where the importance of good, quality extra virgin olive oil (EVOO) in health and wellness is emphasized. This book is a great read for anyone who wants to ensure they have the best quality EVOO, with tips on how to become an at-home taster. As a physician who is passionate about teaching people that *food is medicine,* I honestly believe *Extra Virgin Olive Oil: The Truth in Your Kitchen* will actually make people healthier! It's smart, informative, educational, and entertaining! What an amazing adjunct this will be for all my patients!"

—Orlando V. Gonzalez, MD,
sports medicine and anti-aging specialist,
founder, LIFE*MOD LLC

"'I would like you to warm the cup in your hand, and only after you have done so very carefully, bring the cup to your nose and allow yourself to capture the fragrance of the oil that you will soon experience. Don't look at the color; it may create a bias. Slurp your oil, and it is perfectly fine if you experience a burning sensation and/or cough while doing so.'

This is how David conducted an olive oil tasting event at Yale for over 150 students and staff via Zoom during COVID. Experiential, sensory learning like no other – amazing!

I write this letter of support for our friend and colleague David Neuman, also known as 'EVOO Guy'!

David is, by far, one of the most engaging and informative gastronomic professionals in the space of olive oil. His culinary background, combined with many years of product research and knowledge, enables him to provide the kind of learning that is not abstract but rather applied. David is an excellent source of olive oil information, and we're glad to have him as a friend and subject matter expert in our journey with the Mediterranean diet and olive oil."

—Rafi Taherian,
Associate Vice President, Yale Hospitality

EXTRA VIRGIN OLIVE OIL

THE TRUTH IN YOUR KITCHEN

David M. Neuman

NEW YORK

LONDON • NASHVILLE • MELBOURNE • VANCOUVER

Extra Virgin Olive Oil

The Truth in Your Kitchen

David M. Neuman

Published in New York, New York, by Morgan James Publishing. Morgan James is a trademark of Morgan James, LLC. www.MorganJamesPublishing.com

Proudly distributed by Ingram Publisher Services.

A **FREE** ebook edition is available for you or a friend with the purchase of this print book.

CLEARLY SIGN YOUR NAME ABOVE

Instructions to claim your free ebook edition:
1. Visit MorganJamesBOGO.com
2. Sign your name CLEARLY in the space above
3. Complete the form and submit a photo of this entire page
4. You or your friend can download the ebook to your preferred device

ISBN 9781631957802 paperback
ISBN 9781631957819 ebook
Library of Congress Control Number: 2021947505

Cover Design by:
Rachel Lopez
www.r2cdesign.com

Interior Design by:
Christopher Kirk
www.GFSstudio.com

Morgan James is a proud partner of Habitat for Humanity Peninsula and Greater Williamsburg. Partners in building since 2006.

Get involved today! Visit MorganJamesPublishing.com/giving-back

To all the extra virgin olive oil producers who farm and crush olives early in the harvest every year and bottle their magical oil with quality, authenticity, and beauty as their priorities.

Table of Contents

Acknowledgments xvii
Introduction xxiii

Chapter One | No More Bad Oil For You. 1
Chapter Two | So What the Heck Do I Know?. 19
Chapter Three | Olives & Artisans 37
Chapter Four | What is EVOO really? 61
Chapter Five | What Should I Spend? 81
Chapter Six | Don't Be Duped 93
Chapter Seven | Defects 113
Chapter Eight | Grocery Games 123
Chapter Nine | Whose Opinion Do I Trust? 143
Chapter Ten | Master At-Home Taster, At Last! 157
Chapter Eleven | Your Kitchen, Your EVOO 167
Chapter Twelve | Beat the EVOO Fatigue 191
Conclusion | The Journey Forward 203

Resources You Will Need as an At-Home Taster 207
Brands I Recommend. 211
Where to Find Great Oils. 223
About the Author 225

Acknowledgments

have been fortunate in my long career to have worked with several passionate food entrepreneurs. They have helped mold my philosophy of dogmatic instance on quality, customer service, dedication to never saying no when I knew I was right, and making decisions that were foremost to the benefit of the end consumer, but with a keen awareness to also delivering a return to the investors.

First and foremost, there are two dominant forces in my life, my moral compasses, my only true confidants, as well as the loves of my life. My wife, Semone Neuman, believed in me when many didn't.

She was there for me in the tumultuous days of selling Lucini, starting Gaea, and then leaving it all to go at it on my own. I could tell her anything, ask her everything, and when it

The author and his wife, Semone, at an EVOO event

came to investing our joint retirement funds into my crazy olive oil ideas, she was always my biggest cheerleader. My only child and the apple of my eye, my adult daughter Madeleine, who was around for most of my crazy ride.

The author's wife Semone and daughter Maddie.
(Note: Used with permission by Ron Wood)

She knew when I was away from her for one hundred nights a year to build the businesses I was devoted to, it meant I was working to provide the best life I could for her, as well as deliver results to my employers, peers, and employees. Both Semone and Madeleine have evolved into olive oil snobs, and they spread the gospel to everyone around them.

There are many extra virgin olive oil producers, which I have had the privilege to get to know along this journey, who, in their own way, shaped my ideology of this business. Without the direct contact I have had with them since 2006, I wouldn't be the person I am, nor would this book be possible. Because of what they grow (olives) and bottle (oil), there is an industry for superior grade extra virgin olive oil. Their generosity of access to their estates, mills, warehouses, and even dinner tables have shaped my life and this book.

There are some business allegiances that I cannot leave out, even if they are not in my life today. I may not have always agreed with them, but they all had one thing in common: they all believed in me. Without this trust and—I would argue, love—I would likely still be a chef, anonymously cooking other people's food behind the doors of some commercial kitchen. These names may or may not mean anything to you, the reader, but to me, they are stamps in my life passport and must be mentioned.

- John Hanberry, owner, Beall's 1860 Restaurant (college job)
- Chef Douglas McNeil, master chef, Four Seasons Hotels
- Ann Brody Cove, executive, Sutton Place Gourmet
- Claude Mallinger, director of merchandise, Sutton Place Gourmet
- Bill McGowan, GM, Sutton Place Gourmet
- Joel Dannick, VP Fresh Fields
- Jack Murphy, COO, Fresh Fields
- John Anthony (deceased), VP Sales, Nature's Path
- Arran and Ratana Stephens, founders, Nature's Path Organic
- Art Frigo, Daniel Graeff, Rene Frigo, founders, Lucini Italia
- Cristobal Prat-Gay, President, Molinos Rio La Plata
- Aris Kefolgiannis, founder, Gaea Foods
- Dr. Andrew Weil, founder, Weil Lifestyle
- David Stoup, CEO Weil Lifestyle
- Marcello Scoccia, director of ONAAO
- Tom Mueller, author of *Extra Virginity*

Finally, I would like to thank those who helped me bring this collection of words from ideas and stories to a printed book.

- Morgan James Publishing
- Kim O'Hara, writing coach
- Cortney Donelson, editor
- Carolyn Levin, legal review

Introduction

S pending a few weeks a year during the olive harvest period in a particular country or combination of countries was truly the best benefit of my job as the president of Lucini Olive Oil. Occasionally, my visits coincided with the annual meeting in Rome of the *Flos Olei Olive Oil Guide's* Best Extra Virgin Olive Oil (EVOO) of the Year Ceremony in December. Their annual guide highlights the top 500 producers around the world with special recognition awards for the top twenty brands. After the ceremony, which is always delivered in Italian with direct interpreters, the top twenty brands have a spot on the array of banquet tables where attendees sample their award-winning oils and, with luck, their new harvest. I could connect with producers I admired and people I had come across in my travels. I could also meet new producers of olive oil. I could hardly turn down a sample of gorgeous, aromatic extra virgin olive oil when I strolled by. Those of us close to the industry actually drink olive oil. I have, on many occasions, toasted in a wine glass, with colleagues, freshly made EVOO. How we often taste new oil at harvest time is in the official tulip olive oil tasting glass or on a piece of freshly roasted, dense bread. When the oil connects with the heated bread, the starches accelerate the heavenly aromas and better allow our sense of smell to interpret and assign familiar memories, like freshly cut green grass, tomato leaf, and many more.

However, after tasting twenty of the strongest EVOOs in the world, one can become a bit light-headed and queasy. Polyphenol intoxication, I found, is a real thing. But too much of anything probably is too. I didn't have much of an appetite for solid food after these tasting days, but my palate was having its own orgasm.

Today, I am retired from my corporate endeavors of clocking 150,000 flown miles and 100-plus hotel nights a year to visit extra virgin olive oil producers in Italy, Greece, and Spain and doing battle with big-box retailers over quality, games, and price points. No longer aligned to a big name brand extra virgin olive oil, I am committed full-time to bringing awareness and knowledge to the average consumer of what they are buying on the shelf or online—and how much fraud prevails in this industry. I have a passion to impart my knowledge of what happens from the tree to the store and then to consumers, teaching them how tasting is, at the end of the day, the only defense against buying a bad product.

What makes purchasing olive oil even more complicated for a consumer is that it's not just from Italy, Spain, or Greece anymore. Olive production has taken off in countries that haven't typically been thought of as olive producers: Australia, South Africa, China, Japan, and in the USA, the states of Georgia and Texas are entering the crowded market. I certainly have my favorite cultivars.

What the general public doesn't know is that there are over 900 varieties of olives that can produce olive oil. Italy has 600 of them alone. Most are inedible as an olive even if you brine them. Some cultivars like Manzanilla and Mission, which you likely know, are made into eating olives. With so many different producers, it is even more important than ever to understand the labels on the bottles, learn how to read them, and once again, when you get home and crack that seal . . . know what is acceptable to the palate.

Together, we will go on this informative journey with oil. I will teach you as much as I know to help you have a better experience with olive oil. I have taken every step of the extra virgin olive oil process and made it easy for you to understand, and I will provide some shocking insights—what you see is not always what you get.

CHAPTER ONE

No More Bad Oil For You

Aren't olive oils all the same? If the label indicates the bottle is Italian and it has an Italian name, it's Italian olive oil, right? If it says "Extra Virgin Olive Oil," then that is what I am buying, correct? Are the declarations of health claims on olive oil regulated?

Do these questions sound familiar to you? Have you asked them to grocery store managers, brand ambassadors, or shop owners and been left with a bottle in your hand, feeling like you didn't get the full story or accurate information? You didn't. In my fifteen-plus years in the olive oil business, I have seen consumers receive conflicting information and answers to these questions—and many more—losing the power

1

and choice in their purchasing decisions. When I worked for Lucini Italia Olive Oil, I fought fearlessly to have our high-quality oil stand by its claims, but I saw far and few other brands doing the same. When I left corporate, I could have just retired and moved on, but I had a mission: to be on the ground floor with the consumers and teach them how to take the power back in their olive oil decisions.

I had been in the food industry for thirty years, but as I set up my pop-up olive oil retail shop in a 500-stand weekend farmers' market in the southern US, I finally saw firsthand just how badly consumers needed to be taught how to use EVOO (extra virgin olive oil) and truly know what they are buying. After hundreds of hours working at this shop, I saw that all consumers who came to me to buy or browse were fatigued by conflicting information in this category. They were overwhelmed by the rhetoric, mostly promoted by the media, where olive oil skepticism makes for headlines and readership. The bottom line? Consumers had heard enough. They wanted the truth, and why couldn't we give it to them? I didn't meet one person who wasn't affected by all the emphatic yet egregious statements swirling around. I have said it over five hundred times to consumers in my career: if a bottle or container says the words, "Extra Virgin," it's very likely the contents may not be. Surprised? I would prefer not to start the olive oil journey with you in a tainted manner, but if someone is going to paint a picture of the olive oil marketplace for you, it's going to need to be me. As you get to know me in this book, through my travels and industry trials with the beautiful green elixir called EVOO, you will see why I stepped up to the plate.

It was the very coming together of this farmers' market space that produced a very typical expose of how olive oil is presented to consumers in a "healthy way."

Let me give you the layout. When I first intended to have my eight-foot-by-eight-foot "cage" pop-up shop, the general manager informed me there were two other resellers of olive oil already on the floor. I had to justify why this outdoor market needed a third. Our meeting didn't start well. Prior to our scheduled appointment for my interview, I had scoped out the two other stands that sell olive oil. One, which sold bulk oil in tins, also known as fusties, had the fifty-five-gallon drums of the source olive oil sitting in a corner with a pump in it. I knew the brand name on the big drum, and for me, that was strike one. Olive oil is very volatile to heat, and since I carry my own infrared thermometer, I covertly registered the temperature of that drum of oil at 85°F—far above a safe temperature to store any oil. None of the selling spaces had air conditioning; therefore, rancidity was assured.

The customers had a choice of containers into which to fill the oil. On very dusty shelves sat empty used bottles of everything from Jack Daniels to plastic Coke soda bottles, pickle jars, you name it.

And each container had two things on it: a layer of filth and a price tag. That price is what you were expected to pay to take that grimy container and fill it with "olive oil" from one of the fusties. Strike two.

On a counter made from plywood (an un-cleanable surface, and therefore illegal to use for the public where food is sold), were clear cruet bottles of various oils with open pour spouts

Used bottles in bulk olive oil boutique, fill your own

where the merchant would serve customers a small sample to try. I asked to try a few samples labeled "Extra Virgin." I'll be gentle here and simply say that not only were they not olive oil of any sort, but they were also inedible. This shop had been in that market since the day it opened fifteen years earlier, and locals and visitors had been purchasing and using that "oil" for years. Strike three. I feel sorry for all those consumers who were cheated.

The second shop, a few rows away—the market management wanted to separate stalls with similar items—had many signs declaring, "Made in Italy" and "Best Quality Olive Oil." The shopkeeper, heavyset and already sweaty, glared at me. *How inviting,* I thought. I asked about his brand, which, unlike the first shop, were in bottles with labels. He explained this was his family's land in Italy. However, he was Spanish. Strike one.

I asked to taste the oil. They also had branded bottles opened with a pour spout, allowing all the dirty air swirling around in that market to sneak into the bottles and corrupt the oil. Realizing I would be disappointed again, I took one for the team. The quality was shockingly low. Not EVOO as the label declared. Not even virgin, which is one grade lower. It was full-on *Lampante* ["Lamp Oil" in Italian]—inedible. When I asked the shopkeeper if he knew this oil was bad, he said there was nothing wrong with it. I asked if he knew how to taste oil, and the stare he gave me increased in intensity. Strike two.

I finally asked to purchase a bottle, and he asked me why I wanted a bad bottle of oil. I tried to hide my actual intentions, but I feared he had sniffed me out, so he refused to sell me a bottle. Then I knew I was made. And he knew I had figured out his scam. Strike three.

By the time I walked over to the managers' trailer to have my meeting with the general manager, this sordid fellow, who had just refused to sell to me, was already in the GM's office complaining. Without knowing my name, my skills, or my intentions, he was threatened by my presence and my questions about his quality. If he didn't have something to hide, he wouldn't be so visibly nervous. Isn't this my right as an educated consumer, to ask questions about the food I wish to purchase? The GM called me into his office after concluding with this angry shopkeeper. He murmured to me something to the effect of, "This isn't a good way to start." Well, I took him through my two stall visits before coming to meet with him that morning.

"Would you purchase oil from either of these two shops?" I asked him point-blank.

"No," he immediately replied.

I had made my case for the third stall.

EVOOGuy® farmers market stand

We would be the only one that sold quality and authentic EVOO directly from the estates where it was made. *And* I purchased a commercial glass-door refrigerator, set the temperature to 60°F, the highest it would go, and kept all of my bottles for sale in there. At the safe storage temperature to stave off rancidity. To protect quality. Unlike my "competition." I had a second, smaller commercial fridge, also with a glass door, to hold open bottles of samples that I would pour on demand. This was a shocking change to the existing offerings, and I was met with intense scrutiny by most of the other market shop owners. I mused, "Why is quality always so threatening to other shops?"

Opening my small retail space finally provided me the opportunity to interact with customers face to face. To educate them properly and not just post olive oil philosophy on social media or my website. Prior, I had been testing my face-to-face consumer education and selling skills at public events. Now, my small stand, in a fixed location for weekend business, made it possible for consumers to meet with me in a casual and more food-based shopping setting, which was better suited for having longer exchanges. This store offered interested consumers the ability to meet with me, an expert olive oil taster and executive, and at the same time, be able to taste a variety of great estate EVOOs and make purchase choices from a number of excellent brands that would never be found in grocery stores. I was very proud of the space and what I delivered to the public. In fact, many shoppers, after I opened the stand, returned with family and friends, eager to share their "new find." However, when the patrons asked, "What makes your shop and oil different from the other two at this market?" I had to be *very* careful with my answer. When I signed the vendor agreement at that open-air market, it clearly stated that if I was found to have maligned another stand in the market, I would be asked to leave. So while I very much wanted to talk openly about the cruddy olive oils I found at the other two shops, instead, I simply explained the benefits of mine. Temperature-controlled inventory of both samples and finished goods, samples poured on-demand from fresh bottles, products imported from single estate producers in a curated assortment where I personally know all of the producers, and my experience as a professional taster allowed for an in-depth explanation of both the products and the process of evaluating real EVOO.

All of these differentiators were appreciated by the consumers who visited my stand. They were seeking the truth about authenticity, which was not to be found in the stands of my market competitors. All of my attention to detail, paired with my vast knowledge of olive oil, created a safe space for them to tell me their many heartbreaking stories of misdirection. Shoppers would assume that the olive oil they purchased that stated, "Imported from Italy," meant the olives used to make that oil were indeed Italian, which is what they desired. In fact, when they turned the bottle to the back label, they would find the truth: "May contain oils from Tunisia, Portugal, Chile, Spain, or Italy." Heartbreaking.

I am that passionate about this food. So how does this long history of consumer mistrust end? What should you, as a consumer, do? In our industry, we discuss this fatigue seriously. We fear that if we propagate this, the consumer will run, not walk, in the opposite direction. Seeking to find refuge with other edible fats—butter, Ghee, vegetable oils, coconut oils, and avocado oils. None of which are as healthy for you as a great, fresh, "real" extra virgin olive oil.

This then creates a stifling of the truth, a whitewashing of the issues. *Maybe if we just let this category be, consumers will find a product they will use without any fuss.* The big industrial brands are fine with this. They don't want consumers to ask questions or learn to taste where perhaps their offerings will be less appealing than a better quality brand, which tends to be more expensive. As it rightfully should be. Quality has a price, in everything.

So taking all of the barriers against me into consideration, my goal became, "How can I continue to educate about this product and *not* scare you, the consumer, away?" The answer was to take my message to where the people who care shop. One lesson I came away from the farmers' market stall with was that while some people who shop for fresh produce care about quality EVOO, many don't. This is precisely why the two other stalls that sell unacceptable quality oil survived. The demographics of this market were not strong enough to support a business like mine.

So I decided to test my theory and launched a first-of-its-kind tasting truck. The EVOOGuy Truck—a mobile olive oil tasting event business—would travel throughout the southeastern United States.

I launched this endeavor after much design, planning, and investment. A place where we would speak with hundreds of interested consumers at a time and visit food and wine events, family street fairs, and the like. These eventgoers who found us were seeking to gain more knowledge about what olive oil is, how to judge a good one, and how to use it.

EVOOGuy® mobile olive oil events and store

I had the opportunity to meet with consumers who *do* shop for quality and have the inclination to evolve past the status quo brands they use outside of the typical grocery store environment. This led me to a twenty-store, Florida-wide tasting tour, sponsored by two of my favorite brands, *Mis Raices* and *Casas de Hualdo*, both Spanish family companies who produce their extra virgin olive oils from their land and trees. I coordinated this with a well-respected specialty food retailer. My events were four hours long at each store, and if the weather permitted, I operated them outside in front of the store from my custom olive oil tasting truck. If not, I moved inside with a similar setup.

My focus of the tastings was to interface with consumers using three oils: my two sponsored Spanish products and one Italian organic EVOO from the retailer. These represented various intensities of flavor—bitter and pungent—as well as price points and sizes. And I figured I had two minutes to quickly explain why I was there, teach them some tasting basics, and finally help them select an oil from my tasting assortment that would be good for the household. The findings were telling.

After twenty stores, a few months, and 100-plus hours of face-to-face tastings, every stores' sales had a significant increase during and after my visit that far exceeded what the stores' eight-week average prior sales had been for a week. So if a store had sold two bottles of one of my test oils in the week prior to my visit, during and after my time there, their sales jumped to sixteen bottles in most cases. Sometimes far more.

My conclusion was easy to state but hard to reason. When a consumer is confronted with the opportunity to learn more about a product like EVOO, and if they are the type of shopper who is curious and seeks to gain more knowledge about the food they buy and consume, then after they interface with an expert like me, they *will* change their purchasing habits and buy, in this case, a better and more expensive bottle of EVOO. If you are that same shopper who is breathing out a sigh of relief because you found the guidebook to high-quality olive oil to help you for the rest of your life, welcome. At a given event, I may have seen 200 shoppers walk by me at my set-up over the four hours, but only perhaps twenty-five would stop to visit with me. And of those two and a half dozen, my conversion to a sale was then about 60 percent. Reflecting now after this experiment and event, I am confident that had I been doing this in a region like the northeastern part of the US or another densely populated area with a wider international base of people, my success would have been even higher.

Like these shoppers who went the full nine yards to buy the right oil, you are ready to make changes to the oil in your pantry, but you have some legitimate questions to ask. People I encountered were couples who went on cruises and brought oil back and wanted to know if it's any good. Others were sassy and acted like they knew oil because they needed to feel they have a one-up on me as the seller and that they are relevant. They have been to Morocco and have had local olive oil on hummus. But there were also those who savored a sample of what I was offering, and I could see in their expression that I had answered an age-old question—what should good EVOO taste like? Finally, they were finding out. They overcame their objections to taste oil straight. What I have learned about consumers and olive oil is it can be very polarizing. The way that I approach selling oil is: I don't know who they are until they start to ask me questions. An inquisitive consumer is an educated consumer. And given the complexity of olive oil, an educated consumer is a valuable one to a seller. I see them reading the bottle and I ask, "Is there is anything you want to know that I can help you with?"

They raise their reading glasses, and respond, "No," but that is only because they don't know where to start with their inquiry.

So then I ask, "Is there something, in particular, you are looking for?"

"Oh, I am looking for 'First Cold Pressed' on the label," they will reply. I know this identification is fairly meaningless in determining a quality oil, but they don't.

I will go over this issue and many more in this book. Sometimes, when I correct consumers, they are responsive, but often, they walk away. So I try to put myself in their position and ask a question back that is solution-driven, as I have the opportunity to teach them something new about oil.

I might say, "There are a lot of statements on the bottle I would like to point out to you that are very important." Then I suggest we get inside the bottle and taste the oil. That's where the truth cannot be misdirected by savvy marketing lies.

No question is too embarrassing to ask, and I love any and all questions if it moves people closer to making better olive oil decisions. I am going to provide you with the top ten asked questions of all time, but in reading this book, you will have in a very simple way, gained all the facts behind the production and sales of oil so you can make your own educated buying decision. The endgame is helping you find your great EVOO. You will never have to feel—or be—taken advantage of again.

Frequently Asked Questions I Love to Answer:

1. **Aren't olive oils all the same?**

   Actually no, most are not the same. They vary in degrees of quality of the fruit on the trees, to when that fruit is harvested (and how), when it is crushed and where, how it is crushed, if it's filtered (or not), and then how it's stored, and the methods of packaging, shipping and distribution matter too. (I get into deeper detail on all these processes in Chapter Three). Words of caution: Buyer Beware!

2. **Doesn't all olive oil have to be First Cold Pressed to be legitimate?**

   You are half correct. Virgin olive oil must be made by first crushing the whole olives by mechanical means.

The 'cold' terminology really isn't relevant today. There is a maximum temperature the crushing and separation process cannot exceed, but you would not consider that cold. And olives really aren't pressed anymore—except in rare occasions (stone mills). This terminology is found on almost every bottle of olive oil, primarily for traditional purposes. (See Chapter Four for more on "First Cold Pressed" labeling.)

3. **Is there any benefit in paying more for a brand that states "Extra Virgin" on the label versus a grocery store bottle that declares the same and sells for much less?**

   Yes! With extra virgin olive oil, price matters. The words "Extra Virgin" literally mean that the oil meets the virgin grade but also has met both the chemical and organoleptic standards that indicate the highest grade called "extra virgin." If it's sold for $2 for a 17 oz bottle (500ml), buyer beware! This is hardly extra virgin olive oil. I go into more detail on price, as well as offer resources at the end of the book, including brands I stand by, better retailers, and websites.

4. **If I store my olive oil in the fridge, will it last longer?**
   Not really. It also won't harm the oil. The oil will congeal in the bottle, so prior to use, you will need to let it sit out at room temperature for some time until it has liquified completely. Do *not* run warm water over the bottle to help this process along. For best storage, a cool dark

cabinet, away from the stove or oven is best. I spend a lot of time in Chapter Eleven going over how to store and cook with oil.

5. **I see olive oil displayed in magazines in pretty cruets with a pour spout near the stove for easy access. Why wouldn't I want to have my oil placed in a similar way?**

This is a food styling no-no. It would be akin to leaving your raw chicken out to thaw at room temperature for hours. Leaving olive oil near a hot stove, also perhaps in a clear cruet bottle, with an open pour spout, are sure-fire ways to ruin your olive oil.

6. **The "best before date" on the bottle means the oil remains useable until that date, even if opened?**

No! That date is very much arbitrary. Most bottlers put two years from the date of bottling. And this date *only* applies to bottles that have not been opened. However, many factors can affect the shelf life of any bottle of olive oil based on handling and storage conditions. And once you open a bottle, any bottle, you should use the oil up as fast as possible. The higher the quality of the oil, the longer it may last. As a rule of thumb, try to finish a bottle in less than two months. (In Chapter Eight, I go into all the pitfalls and games of labeling in grocery stores . . . again, buyer beware!)

7. **How many bottles of oil can one expect from a large tree?**

   This varies depending on the cultivar of olive as well as the amount of sun the tree receives. But on average, based on my experience, it is typically five bottles of 17 oz high-quality EVOO. That's only 2.5 liters.

8. **Is there really a difference between clear bottles and dark bottles? I want to see the oil. I hear green oil is better.**

   There is a *big* difference between the two. Olive oil will experience a change with exposure to light. This photosynthesis changes the oil and creates rancidity quickly. Rancidity, as you will learn in this book, is a defect that disqualifies any bottled labeled as extra virgin grade olive oil from using that descriptor. Dark glass has UV light protection and prevents most light (if dark glass) to no light (if the bottle is painted or wrapped) from getting through. Therefore, the quality is easily more assured when a bottle is tinted to reduce light from entering and damaging the contents. Green oil can be wonderful. If the green is a natural result of the olives and not if it has been dyed that color. But great EVOO doesn't have to be naturally green to be great. I have had many wonderful yellow oils (not orange).

9. **I have an opened bottle of olive oil, how long will it be good for?**

   This can be a loaded question. But let me attempt to answer it. The answer is fluid, as we don't know the quality of the oil you started with nor if it had nitrogen in the package prior to opening it to protect the quality and better manage the shelf life. A smaller bottle can last longer than a larger container because of the size of the space in the package that is exposed to air once the package/bottle is opened, poured from, and then re-sealed. If I were considering a really great bottle of oil, kept in a dark cool pantry closet, in a dark glass (not plastic) bottle, I estimate that the oil would be usable for a few months—no more than that. (Have old oil? You'll find out in Chapter Eleven what to do with it.)

10. **I use olive oil for my health—isn't it true that all olive oils provide the same health benefits?**

    No way is the short answer. Many social media influencers, some brands, and many would-be nutrition "experts" would have you believe that a specific olive oil is better than others, while some will just say olive oil is a healthy fat-loaded food with anti-inflammatory properties and antioxidants that lowers cholesterol, etc. These two positions alone are very confusing because they are so dissimilar. The reality is the FDA is very specific about what can be legally conveyed to a consumer about the benefits of olive oil and health. Many brands disregard this, post misinformation on their websites, and even add illegal claims to their bottles. Yes, great EVOO is a healthy fat. One of the only fats that actually does have health benefits. But this is all contingent on many factors, which you will learn about in the following chapters of this book.

As we dive into the world of olive oil, you don't have to be an aficionado to take in what I am going to share with you about olive oil. Knowing the origin of the oils, the condition of the harvest, management of the oil while in bulk storage, the quality of the packaging, the time the oil took en route to the US or stores, and much more are essential to your shopper wellbeing. Once you read this book, you will never have to be misled about olive oil again. This book is meant to empower you, the reader, to make better decisions when you shop for or use EVOO when out of the house. The power comes from knowledge. Now, let's get smart about EVOO.

EVOO FAST FACTS:

Olive oil is an edible fat. Not a juice. Olive oils are classified very differently by the FDA. We all need healthy fats in our diet. Fat is the fuel our brains use the most for the energy they need. Changing the fats in your diet from saturated (processed and animal) to monounsaturated (like olive oil) means you are eating healthier while still getting to enjoy what you eat.

CHAPTER TWO
So What the Heck Do I Know?

F irst, go right into your pantry and take a look at all the bottles of olive oil that you believe you have had for six months or longer. Do some of them have a layer of dust and grime on the bottle from lack of use? Is that once-lovely sundried tomato-infused oil, a gift from so long ago you can't even recall who gave it to you, still in there? Or how about the bottles you have bought in a moment of confusion in the grocery store aisle just to get the heck out of the section. Get a big box because we are going to throw most of them in the dumpster. But save a few because, in Chapter Seven, we are going to learn how to smell defects, and if you don't think your oil is rancid enough, just put it in a sunny window for a couple of days and mismanage it like most grocery stores and restaurants. Then you will discover what *rancid* truly smells and tastes like. You won't soon forget it.

We are starting anew.

In the sixteen years since I was recruited into a senior-level executive role in the extra virgin olive oil industry, I have explored and experienced every facet—the good, bad, and ugly—with this oil that is often labeled as a "commodity," no matter what country it is from. I have also seen that extra virgin olive oil has a groupie-like following, one that I became a member of in my time learning the magic of its creation. Those of us in love with real extra virgin olive oil, the highest grade, truly love its history and its many uses. Many consumers use extra virgin olive oil (or so labeled) but are unaware that what they are buying may not truly be the real deal. Knowing the truth behind a defect-free, properly labeled extra virgin olive oil can change their lives—and yours—in fundamental ways.

Heavy consumers of olive oil who buy the cheap kind for the value or convenience need to know what they are actually buying is basically a tasteless, possibly mislabeled product, and they should have an idea of where, how, and why the standards are broken in the production and distribution chains. Since you are reading this book, you have a desire to know more about the oil you put on your food and serve to your family. I have purposely made this process a simple one—an overview education and a class in tasting. I will outline the possible fraud with labeling and grocery games, having been in the food industry for the last thirty years, as well as share experiences I have had in some of the most beautiful olive farms in the world.

I know you have had to operate in a world where you're often told false truths about the oil in your cabinet, and now I am asking you to trust me to not lead you astray. And you might be asking, "Who the heck does this guy think he is?" I once was like you. I knew very little about olive oil, and I was definitely a grab-and-go shopper. But I have had a passion for food since childhood.

My foodie proclivities were first tantalized when I worked at Willams Sonoma in the late 1980s in Alexandria, Virginia, in a part-time job. Not just to earn more money (at the time, I think I made six dollars an hour), but the 50 percent discount meant a lot to a young man who loved to cook but couldn't afford the cookware. I loved the different aspects of the high-end pots and pans and the unique smallwares, such as the garlic presses and paring knives. Almost every week, I returned to my apartment with some odd piece of cooking equipment and have toted them around from house to house and city to city over the last forty years. They also sold what I believed at the time to be curated and expensive olive oils, tucked away in a shelving display in the corner of the store. I never purchased any of them, since they were over $20 a bottle at the time. Today, they are even higher. But it did give me pause, and I thought, "If Williams Sonoma carried them, there must be something to super-premium olive oil." Little did I know at the time that EVOOs would become the largest part of my life's work.

My management pursuits launched at the Four Seasons Hotel in Washington D.C. in 1985, after college, as I took on a tough internship as a Comis Chef and then transitioned into the front of the house as "Lounge Management." That year, in a world-class kitchen—working for a Master Chef and cooking food for the likes of Adnan Khashoggi, Queen Noor, and Michael Jackson—was formative for my interest in superior quality ingredients. But years of hotel life taught me that perhaps specialty food retail was better suited for a married man. Fewer hours and nights. Or so I thought. I worked incredibly hard at three high-end food retailers: Sutton Place Gourmet (today called Balducci's), Fresh Fields Market, and their acquiring company, Whole Foods Markets—all of which were, for a number of years, capitalizing on the growth of eating better and healthier foods.

In 1996, I finally had enough of retail and was discovered by Nature's Path Foods, a small, family-run, organic cereal producer based in Vancouver, BC, Canada. They saw me as their first foray into the US natural foods craze being led by my employer at the time, Whole Foods. The decision changed the course of my life and professional endeavors. While I knew I was far more committed to specialty foods, having been exposed to them for so many years, learning about a food trend from the manufacturing and product development side was very intriguing to me.

Being hired by the founder at Nature's Path was flattering and scary at the same time. But what really helped me evolve out of my shell was when I participated in the creative part of the business. The team was small, but that allowed me to really throw out some crazy new product ideas—many of which stuck, and you will still find them selling on shelves today. Like Optimum Power Breakfast cereal, which I ideated while out for a long run on a warm D.C. Saturday. The first of its kind was is an organic cereal to support active consumers who needed a well-rounded breakfast post-workout. That product became the #1 best-selling cereal in the natural foods industry in the US and Canada in its first year on the market. Even Costco had it for sale in jumbo boxes.

Beyond cereal, my creative juices helped launch a kids' line of organic snack bars and hemp granola (which ran into a lengthy legal challenge during the George W. Bush administration, but a few years later, the hemp industry prevailed in the circuit court) and the first-ever organic "toaster pastry" (think healthy Pop-Tarts). We launched over one hundred new items during my formative years there. Over the ten years I built that business, my team and I—and the industry as a whole—grew to understand that A) I needed to work with a food that is used to cook with and enjoyed over many meal periods, not just at breakfast, and B) I am a stickler for quality and authenticity.

So when Lucini Italia Extra Virgin Olive Oil started to woo me, I was willing to consider the leap into a new area of specialty food I knew nothing about. How much more complex could it be than organic food? Boy, did I rue those words!

What follows is the tale of how an Ashkenazi Jew from Washington, D.C., who didn't speak any Italian, Greek, or Spanish, got involved with olive oil. First, there was a corporate recruiter from Miami. She tricked her way to my desk (through the cereal company's receptionist) and told me she was a fan of my work; she ate the foods I helped create every morning. Apparently, this was more than a year-long retained search for the first president of a family business who needed someone who could fit into the family dynamics with a subtle hand to push the business ahead and not rock any boats.

A few months later, during this recruitment process, in March of 2006, I left for my annual pilgrimage to Anaheim, California, to the largest health food show in the world: Natural Products Expo West. All the biggest health trends percolated here—Smart Water, Cliff Bars, Kashi, White Wave Soy Milk, Stoneyfield yogurt, and many more. We had a company eighteen-wheeler parked down the street from the Anaheim Convention Center, adorned on both sides with our brand name/logo, product images, etc. That alone was a $10,000 sponsorship. Plus, we had a tent in front of the show entrance with young people handing out samples of our newest creations to the thousands of attendees.

At the end of day three of the show, after long dinners with customers and hundreds of booth-side chats (including with celebrities, such as Ed Begley Jr, Daryl Hannah, Dr. Andrew Weil, and other notables), I was wrung out. I retired to my hotel before our last team dinner, and upon entering, discovered sitting on the table next to the kitchenette, a large, attractive glass bottle of what seemed to be olive oil. How odd, I thought. I had never seen that brand. I didn't know a thing about olive oil. I searched around for a card, thinking maybe it was a gift from the hotel manager. I thought, "What am I going to do with a bottle of olive oil?" I was flying home in the morning and didn't want to take a chance packing it. Most of us remember the pre-9/11 days, where we could carry liquids on board the airplane.

I made the decision to leave it in my room, figuring a housekeeper might enjoy it. I still left my monetary tip, as always. The name of that olive oil was Lucini Italia. I made a mental note to remember it. It looked good. But what did I know?

Lucini Italia Tuscan and Southern Italia EVOO (2006–2015)

It turns out the recruiter who had called me and begun her head-hunting had it placed there. She, on behalf of the company, had been spying on me at the show . . . to examine my effectiveness, I suppose. These revelations sprang into action a thirty-day expedited interview process that involved three trips to Miami, the headquarters for Lucini Italia. Meeting the father of the angel investor of Lucini at The Ritz was followed by a private interview session with the very famous right-brained marketing guru, Dr. Kenny, who was hired to dig into my mind and see how I would handle the newfound responsibilities and stresses. I appreciated the thoroughness of the process.

The interview process continued, but now in first-class on United Airlines from Chicago to Seattle. A former CEO who worked for the angel investor of Lucini was on his way to play golf with the founder of Costco, and the owners wanted his opinion of me. I eagerly acquiesced to a review in the friendly skies. Unfortunately, I was placed on a different side of the plane, and neither of our seatmates would move. They both had aisle seats, which I agree are more comfortable. I could see my wonderful opportunity fading away but knew if I could solve this dilemma, I could possibly gain an additional feather in my cap. So I actually begged the gentleman next to me. I explained I was interviewing for the job of a lifetime. And United had made a mistake and mis-seated us. I was thinking of what else I could offer him. But I finally wore him down, and he made the switch. I don't remember his name anymore, but I will never forget his graciousness. That trip was a very productive four hours.

I was working my tail off to gain access to the wonderful world of extra virgin olive oil without even having dialed in yet to how passionate I would be about this green elixir.

The Lucini founders' generosity of the offer certainly made the opportunity more attractive. My larger fear wasn't the change in food from cereal to olive oil, or from the Pacific Northwest to Miami, but it was about product price. The average selling price to the consumer of the breakfast foods I had worked with for the last ten years was $4. With Lucini, the average selling price for their products was $15. That three times multiple really worried me. It would be like going from selling Hyundai to Mercedes cars. Yes, people drive both. But the audience for the Mercedes is a lot smaller and a lot harder to reach. I was moving from a company with sales north of $100 million a year to $5 million—from highly profitable to not yet profitable. But there was one remaining question I had to finalize my decision. And it was directed at me. *Did I like the* taste *of the Lucini Italian*

Tuscan EVOO better than *the taste of the organic breakfast cereals, toaster pastries, granola bars, and waffles that I had been developing and selling for the last ten years?*

Did I mention I don't eat cereal and never have?

When I gave the CEO of the number-one, best-selling organic cereal brand in the US and many other countries, including Canada (their hometown), my resignation to take on olive oil, his parting words to me were: "Be careful. Lightning doesn't strike twice in the same place."

The olive oil I had been personally using as a novice cook was an off-the-shelf grab. Like most people, I knew nothing about the very oil I put on my food. How could I be so naïve? I had been in the food business for fifteen years by then, yet understanding extra virgin olive oil had never been on my radar. Until this job, I fell into the same rabbit hole as most consumers; I believed oils were all the same. Italian-sounding names, images of peasants on the label, and price were all arbiters of authenticity. I knew everything about being "organic." That's a quality standard and one with legal parameters.

I went into hyper-speed education mode. I asked Lucini to send me some industry data so I could begin to educate myself about the category before I started. I also hit up my food brokers and the syndicated market data group, SPINS, to help provide me with category information. What brands sold, why, and for how much? I realized early on that there are two vital points to this. First, there is a race to the bottom on price. The lower the price, the better a brand did. And secondly, there were no serious brands above $15 a bottle (17 oz) to speak of. Lucini was there but barely. Low quality, low price, and private labels drove the category. That left me with a slightly panicked feeling about that lightning not striking twice comment. *How would I make an expensive product in an idle category a success?*

Still, I had committed, and I was all in to learn what I could from my own experience and observations as president and partner. For the next nine years, I traveled easily one million miles. I spent over 500 nights in hotels. And as a result, Lucini Italia became the #1 best-selling olive oil brand despite that elusive $15 a bottle (17 oz) and held that spot for many years, reaching new consumers all over the US and Canada. And yes, even in the local Haggen's stores in Bellingham, Washington, where I had lived for years while at Nature's Path. I learned everything I know about olive oil in those miles and trips with the many purveyors and distributors, but it was also in the sky that I connected directly with the consumers and heard the consistency of their confessions: "I just buy what looks good on the shelf."

I have spent countless hours with fellow airline passengers, giving olive oil lessons. Once it surfaces that I am an "olive oil guy," which is ultimately why my business is called EVOOGuy. com®, flight attendants, hoteliers, and fellow guests quickly express their desire to know more about what extra virgin olive oil really is and how to know if they have bought a decent brand. With limited time to interact with these folks, and in an effort to both not bore them nor turn them off from using extra virgin olive oil, I summarized a few behind-the-scenes nuggets. I also spoke a bit about my brand, which usually concluded with offering them one of the "Free Item" coupons I always carried in my bag. A gentle incentive to go to the store and *not* purchase just any olive oil, but to try mine, a truly amazing one. But the path to getting healthy, fresh, glorious EVOO to them is far more interesting than they know or you as a reader understand . . . yet. It's a journey riddled with obstacles, challenges, deceit, and expense but also passion and downright pleasure.

I enjoyed countless memorable meals in Italy during my frequent visits to tour the olive oil producers we contracted to produce the Lucini EVOO. I toured some of the best wineries in the world, like Gaja, Sassicaia, and Ornellaia. I even made it to the dairy where the Queen of England sources her yogurt. And I became an officially-trained olive oil taster. What affected me the most, more than any reality I had encountered in all my years of working in the food biz, was that olive oil is a completely broken industry, rife with challenges and consumer confusion and apathy. I knew I had to do something to rework and distribute the information, even if it was in my own, small way. I couldn't leave unfinished business.

So that's me in a nutshell, and I am now committed to educating you, the consumer, in the production of extra virgin olive oil—good, honest, real-quality olive oil that takes true effort and commitment from everyone responsible for its production. From the tending of the very tree the olives grow upon to the stocking of bottles on the store shelves. While many consumers who are educated in quality EVOO can be crowned as "hip foodies" by their friends and families, I see that small margin as too little. Everyone should know the true value of EVOO, and you don't have to be a "foodie" to understand. Once you have opened your eyes (and senses) to the true pleasures of EVOO, how you eat will change forever.

Olive oil is one of the most tampered with foods in the marketplace today. Just Google: "most mislabeled foods," and see what comes up. "How can that be?" you say, "with all the restrictions and labeling requirements in place to protect us as consumers?" Ah! More to come, but I can assure you, there is a buried history, which most commercial olive oil companies don't wish consumers to know about. That's because EVOO, an unrefined, all-natural oil, as well as a raw food, is very simply the olives crushed and minimally processed into edible oil and bottled, versus olive oil (Pure, Lite), which is refined, blended, and "fixed," using an array of unpleasant but necessary methods. EVOO is a complex food, more so than you likely realize. A magical elixir. But you don't have to be a magician to know how to determine for yourself what is real and what may be adulterated.

The plan for the founders of Lucini when they interviewed me was threefold: grow the business, make it profitable, and sell the business within ten years. When Lucini sold to California Olive Ranch in late 2014, I thought my time working for oil companies was done. I had accomplished what the Lucini founders had asked. But soon after, I was called by the founder of Gaea Products of Greece to launch a subsidiary, Gaea North America, LLC, and become the CEO.

I spent the next three and a half years building another brand of premium extra virgin olive oil, olives, and other Greek specialties in the US market. Changing gears from a truly beautiful Italian EVOO to representing a Greek brand took some adaptation. EVOO is different in every region. Gaea was a bottler of their oil but not a producer. This provided more quality control in one sense, but given their dependency on thousands of farmers

Gaea Greek EVOO (2015–2018)

and many co-op(erative) mills to process the olives, great annual harvest variations resulted. This challenged my sensibilities.

Lucini never produced its oils but had tight relationships with the estates that crushed the olives and stored the oil. Having become a talented taster allowed me the skills to better evaluate the oils that each annual production provided, and I was vocal to the Gaea owner about any variations that I felt could be detrimental to the market. This is uncommon for a senior executive to do. But given the fragility of the US olive oil marketplace, I felt it was incumbent of me to have this capability. During my short time at Gaea, I was able to develop many products in cooperation with the parent company. From entry-level quality and price to the best oil and highest price we could achieve. And we had decent products. But my snobbery around olive oil quality had really started to take over, and I was desperate to work with even better quality oils than what I had with both the Lucini and Gaea brands. My palate had grown and having now had access to hundreds of olive mills around the world and tasted some of

Author at a harvest in Toledo, Spain, with green olives
Used with permission by Cristina Aizpun Vines

the best EVOOs made, my passion to share this knowledge with consumers was the highest it had ever been.

The big questions were "how" and "when" could I make this transition? The "when" would be answered for me sooner than I expected.

Ultimately, the financial woes of Greece that started and hit hard in 2015, right when we launched the new US subsidiary, were too much for the company and their board to handle after a few years. No matter how much revenue we created or retail placements we achieved, it wasn't enough for them. In early 2018, they decided to close the Gaea USA office that I had opened. The "when" had arrived. I enjoyed having had another kick at the can running another olive oil brand. But I was ready for a break.

In May 2018, I started on my own journey. This time I would be my own boss. EVOOGuy.com® was born.

We all need beauty in our lives. Each of us defines what *beauty* means to us. Some relish a special tattoo. Others, a particular hairstyle. There are those who prefer more tangible bangles like a special timepiece. To a foodie, there are "beautiful" elements to cookware, appliances, and food ingredients, that when used together, typically produce a memorable meal that nourishes our souls. It became my mission to add beautiful quality, authentic EVOO to that list of must-haves in every home.

During the COVID-19 health crisis of 2020, we all took a closer look at those beautiful items we could bring into our homes because we weren't going out to eat as much, not traveling, and hunkering down and trying our best to overcome grief by exploring different foods, hobbies, and even a new frame of mind about the foundation of our future. Our essence of where we come from—the land, the trees, the soil—was made more significant. Consumerism took off. People spent money on discretionary items, such as high-end bicycles, boats, kayaks, RVs, and even cars. And yes, grocery stores sold products at record levels. The US olive oil industry which usually saw 1–2 percent annual growth, recorded over 20 percent year-over-year sales increases. So, spending 50 percent more (from $6.99 to $13.99 for 500 ml) on a bottle of "real" EVOO doesn't seem like such a stretch for most.

If you have not made that stretch, let's assume you didn't have the insight and knowledge to know why you should. My intention is to lead you to a place where you see only buying true extra virgin olive oil as acceptable for you and your household as part of the necessary beauty in your kitchen and the nutritional balance for your family. I also hope it is not acceptable for you to be lied to by producers who claim they are selling you something they are not. It makes me angry to know that consumers are being taken for a ride, but I know that knowledge is the key—and the best retaliation. I don't expect you to be an accredited expert by the time you are done reading this book, but you will understand the beautiful process of how olive oil is made and be equipped with a simple system and process to be a smart and happy olive oil consumer. Your days of confusion at the olive oil shelves are over. Let's get on with the education, shall we?

EVOO FAST FACTS:

- Olive oil is one of the oldest known foods, dating back 6,000 years to Greece!

- Olive oil was so valuable in Ancient days, it used to be traded for currency and was a prize for winning in the Olympics.

CHAPTER THREE

Olives & Artisans

Extra virgin olive oil starts with the trees and healthy olives, properly farmed, picked, crushed, separated, and bottled. As a novice to extra virgin olive oil, or perhaps as a tourist in Italy, you can look at sweeping olive groves or mills and think, "Oh, that is so beautiful and lovely. I bet the most amazing olive oil is produced there."

Yes and no. Extra virgin olive oil can be quantified by simple math: the input (good fruit) equals the output (quality oil). The producers start with pruning, to entice the trees to generate new branches, which will sprout new flowers, ultimately becoming olive fruit. It sounds relatively simple. A tree grows a stone fruit; it is picked once a year, and that fruit goes to a mill to be crushed. That's what I thought when I started in this industry. Boy, was I wrong. The way a farm looks from the roadside or how they market their oil means little to nothing if the production process cuts corners. I am here to inform you that many producers cut corners, and those oils are predominately found on supermarket shelves.

Olive oil is sourced in many different countries, and the quality of the work that goes into growing the olives, picking the fruit, crushing it, storing it, and ultimately bottling it matters. A lot. I understand you are busy and don't have time to think about olive oil trees or production, but you are making the effort to buy olive oil to put on your food. Knowing if it was produced with care can be part of your purchasing and decision-making process versus being lied to or rooked by labels that indicate good production practices. You wouldn't serve your family spoiled meat, right? Well, much of the oil that sits on the store shelves may be bad, or at the least, mislabeled. Either way, it's not what you expect it to be.

Good olive oil starts with the tree. I refer to quality farmers, bottlers, or millers as artisans of oil. Keepers of the gates to the olives. Because what they make is art. Edible art. And they are passionate about it. They listen to the trees as their gastronomic muse, some as old as 1,000 years, still producing usable olive fruit.

They have survived wars, droughts, earthquakes, lightning strikes, and insect damage. The older the tree, the more complex the fruit. The less help a farmer or grower gives to the tree to aid its production of fruit, the better the resultant oil will be. The trees grow in many climates in dozens of countries. If you travel and get to see olive groves first-hand, you will be able to iden-

Author harvesting Empeltre olives in Spain
Used with permission by Victor Moreno Pastor

tify the olive trees pretty easily. With their long, narrow, silvery leaves that shimmer, the fruit—usually green but can also be purple and, in some cases, black—like small jewels hanging off branches, waiting for their fateful destiny.

The harvesting of the olives every fall/winter in the Northern Hemisphere can be as simple as picking by hand (a.k.a., the traditional method), hand-assisted (with a battery operated picker with rotating "fingers"), tree-shaken (where a Boogie machine grabs a tree trunk and shakes the fruit onto nets waiting beneath the tree), or medium- or high-density picking, which utilizes harvester trucks so one man can pick acres of trees (grown on flat land) an hour by himself.

Personally, I like the romance of the more traditional methods. For the quality producers, the less damage to the olive fruit and the earlier in the harvest the fruit is picked and crushed, the better the resultant oil will be. But this latter process, while ideal, can't make enough oil for those who wish to upgrade to a better product, nor sell for the abhorrent low prices you see today for typical olive oil. My local grocery store has a "Buy one, get one free (BOGO)" promotion every week on some brand of supermarket oil. Mix and match any type that brand produces for $7.99 (for two 17 oz bottles). Trust me, these oils were not hand-picked from the tree. In fact, the methods used are not with quality in mind but rather, volume.

The artisans' resultant olive oil is a green liquid that streams out of the centrifuge, the final production stage, after a quick but thorough run through an expensive mill, gleaming with the best equipment. If you start with the very best "art" that you can (e.g., the olive), then the chances of a consumer thousands of miles away receiving and experiencing their masterpiece with delight are far greater than if you produce the lowest quality oil possible, for the sake of volume and low price.

Once the olive is picked off the tree (not the ground, but the lower-priced products do use dropped fruit that is vacuumed up for use) the quality clock is ticking. Unlike balsamic vinegar, for instance, the quality of olive oil cannot ever get better (unrefined). Olive trees grow in both the Northern and Southern Hemispheres. And olive trees date back over 4,000 years. Many say longer. They are one of our oldest recorded foods. And there are many ways they grow—either wild, on land where the trees have stood for hundreds of years or longer, or on managed olive groves, where more modern farming methods have improved the yield and speed of harvest with machinery versus being hand-picked.

The trees I have bought oil from are typically very old. Some producers are making oil out of very young trees that have been damaged by aggressive harvesting and repurposed. Years ago, while on an international olive harvest trip, I visited a very large EVOO producer. I was given an all-access pass to how they are vertically integrated from starting an olive tree in a greenhouse to the very harvesters, which they custom-built, used to pick the olives.

This producer spends years growing a small olive plant inside the controlled greenhouse until it has matured enough to be planted in a nice straight row with others. Then it will take a few more years before it bears fruit.

After learning a lot about their "secret sauce" of farming, what I was shocked by, was an explanation about damage to the trees during harvest. After the enormous harvester passes over the row of trees, where three huge olive trees end up inside this machine and spinning, sturdy "fingers" are knocking the olives

Author visiting medium-high density (MHD) olive grove

off of the branches into awaiting conveyors, which hurry them out of the harvester, over the row of trees, and into a waiting dump truck. There is a lot of damage to the branches when the harvester exits. This makes sense given the assault to the tress this harvester creates. Behind the harvester is a "tree ambulance" with agronomists who will prune damaged branches away and spray a cocktail of tree medicines to prevent the harvesting damage from killing the tree. While I can intellectually understand damage occurs, and trees need to be saved, it seems hard to imagine a quality fruit can be produced with such intense harvesting techniques being employed. In some cases, the trees cannot be saved. In these instances, a new tree is brought in from the greenhouse to replace it. But, in fact, this producer does make a decent oil. However, it's not as beautiful as any EVOO I have experienced from smaller, hand-harvested trees.

If you want to understand good and bad olive oil, you have to learn how it is made. Based on the heritage of the area, old production methods still exist, such as using granite stones to crush the olives and mats to press the oil. And in some countries, like Greece, antiquated harvest techniques are still popular because the older farmers refuse to evolve, and their concern for quality isn't foremost on their minds. For the brands I was associated with, we worked with producers who combine generations of experience but utilize modern milling equipment. To ensure quality, the early harvest fruit must be crushed as soon as possible to ensure a high quality of oil, typically within hours of being crushed. The oils are usually crushed on the estate where the olives grow or at a local mill nearby. Time is of the essence. Every moment that escapes after the olives were picked means less and less quality. The olives are de-leaved at the entrance of the mill, then usually washed well and air-blade dried. I worked with a mill owner in Cordoba, Spain, who had built his own invention of an olive "Jacuzzi" to disturb the olives using bubbling water to get them good and clean. Then they were moved on a conveyor belt to the crushing phase, most times with the pits still in them.

There are a few options that are widely used for crushing, but the most popular are hammer mills (that beat the olives to a pulp) or rotating knives. The pits are separated and dried, and the better millers utilize these for fuel. The next step is for the paste exiting the crush to go to the malaxer.

Imagine a giant mix master that "kneads" the olive paste at a temperature lower than 23°C. And the less time this takes, the better. Typically, a good producer will malax for thirty minutes.

Malaxer at work separating EVOO from water and solids

From there, the paste is separated into three parts: grey water, the solids, and what remains is olive oil. The final step is using a centrifuge that spins away any remaining water drops, leaving unfiltered olive oil.

Since the oil hasn't been graded yet, the producer can't say that it is extra virgin. Depending on the quality of the fruit, the processing methods, and the ethics of the producers, it could very well be. The oil is sent to stainless steel silos where it is stored. Better producers pump nitrogen into the headspace of the silo, which displaces air to better protect the oil from aging (oxidation). Producers aren't required to declare this on their label. Only a handful of the superior ones do. In most cases, the oil will sit for about a month to allow the sediment to separate and fall to the bottom of the silo. This is referred to as "racking."

Then the oil is pumped out to a filtration area where it is forced through cellulose filters, which strain out the solids and any remaining water. The result is clear olive oil. This oil is sent to a clean silo for storage until bottling or bulk packing, which should again be nitrogen-flushed. Under good conditions, where the silos are maintained in either a temperature-controlled warehouse or are jacketed and cool water is circulated then topped with nitrogen, the filtered oil should last a year. It will likely be bottled before then. And the "best before date" is almost always eighteen to twenty-four months from the date of bottling.

I have visited a lot of harvests over the years. I have seen what can go wrong and what can go very right. You may get olive oil, and it's from these beautiful trees, but the process that turns olives into EVOO can unfold in a factory that is often unclean, with people working under no sanitation standards, using no hair nets, wearing no gloves, and pouring the oil into vats with no tops. I have seen this for myself on visits to mills and bottling operations.

Olive oil is a special and romantic food, but I am here to pull the curtain back. At the tree phase, everything is lovely and healthy and mostly sanitary. Minutes later, when the fruit is placed on the truck and headed to those factories, all bets are off. There are producers who take pride in their work and have beautiful mills. Many have good manufacturing practices (GMPs) but many do not. The truth lies in their efforts and always ends up in the oil they make. I can tell the differences instantly, and in some lesser ways, you will too.

When you have worked for some of the better brands of EVOO, you have varying experiences on your trips to harvest. On one of my harvest trips working for Lucini, I was taking a rare peek into the private estates owned by one of the multi-generational families of olive oil royalty. The Pizzone Family had been producing olive oil on the same family land in the Tuscan hills for hundreds of years. I was always of interest to producers of great oil because when I was with Lucini, I contracted for hundreds of thousands of liters of quality EVOO a year. To visit this family, I would arrive in Pisa, usually, and then drive from Livorno, where our supply office was, to the countryside in Reggello, in the hills above Florence. The original mill was partially intact under a newer building and had been turned into a museum for visitors. Also residing on their hillside property was an ancient and still utilized church. On their land and in neighboring groves, much of the olive oil I was charged with selling in America originated. To say I was somewhat intimidated is an understatement. I was buying the oil and making a decision. This is instrumental in pricing the product and establishing quality.

Despite the romanticism of the location and the relationships I had built, I needed to be discerning because some years, they had produced great oil, and other years, I had to bounce orders to other producers. I have to remain true to my ultimate goal, which is to return with the highest quality oil available for that particular harvest.

Olive oil is an agricultural product. The producers are not making steel screws and nails. The quality can vary due to such challenges as inclement weather, pests, and drought. The news is not always wonderful in Italy. In a hard year, you pay for these trees' upkeep for a year, and then they only produce half the usual yield. I would feel guilty not taking orders after blind tastings with them. They may cook up the one sample bottle I taste to evaluate and approve, and then switch up the oil used for my branded oil for the finished production. I visited these producers multiple times in a year—once in February to look at the pruning and then in the spring when the trees were flowering, which is an indicator of how well the fruit is expected to be. More flowers mean more fruit because the flower becomes the fruit. My job is to make sure the oil in these bottles is good, so I had to be part of the whole process!

When the harvest time arrives in the Northern Hemisphere, late September if it's too warm but most likely in early October for the quality producers, I hopefully bask in the unabashed simplicity of oil, the first cold press of truly amazing olives, after almost a year of flowing, fruiting, and growing to the point of harvest. Grass-green *olio novello*, the first run, exits the centrifuge and we taste that fresh, pure oil. There is little in the food world that is so wonderful, so versatile.

Olio Novello, the fresh stuff at harvest, not filtered

I was very fastidious, passionate, and dedicated to understanding the oil that the brand I represented produced. My circles were with small family producers, and I rarely ran into the industrial cooperatives that would ship their oil in tankers. Yet, one still had to be on their toes when presenting oil to buyers and media writers, who I took as my guests every year during harvest when I worked for Gaea. The same mill could be making your oil one way and another brand's oil another. You have to clarify the oversight because this is a local, cooperative mill, and they really don't have any skin in the game.

One very vivid memory for me was a harvest trip to Crete, Greece in 2016 with notable buyers of oil, such as Kehe Distributors, Rainbow Co-Op, Meijer, and journalists representing *Huffington Post, Food and Wine, Good Housekeeping, Bloomburg Business,* and *Grocery Headquarters* (who wrote a great story about our Greek trip). My goal was for them to experience the heritage of making olive oil for my brand, to visit the trees, observe the picking, and tour the mills where my EVOO was born.

My biggest hope was for these decision-makers and writers to witness, first-hand, that olive oil can be—*and is*—made often by much smaller producers who create an entirely different product than the commercial products found on grocery store shelves. I wanted to share also how Greek oil makers can vary from responsible to a much lower standard than I would ever endorse. If I were to show my guests the correct methods, I needed to also warn them of what they may witness with less than ideal transporting and processing practices. This starts with the fruit—the earlier the harvest, the more green the fruit. Green fruit typically produces a more intense olive oil. Often this can also mean it's higher in polyphenols, the healthy stuff we all expect from EVOO. Depending on when we can get to the harvest and the climate, the fruit could have already started to turn purple or even black. The darker the color, the more ripe the fruit is and consequently, the less intense is the flavor, with the possibility of some defects.

Beyond the fruit being picked or swept up off the ground, many of the Greek farmers that my group encountered that trip use jute (cloth) sacks to transport the olives to the mill. Ideally, they would use plastic bins with open sides to allow the fruit to breathe. These sacks have been used by Greeks for thousands of years, as they are ideally suited to hold fruit picked on hilly terrain for easy transport.

Sad sacks of olives at harvest in Greece (Crete)

But they are terrible for the oil. If it is a very large grove, a dump truck is loaded with the newly-picked fruit and taken to the mill. We did see the sacks—and I forewarned my group that these were *not* the olives we used at Gaea.

I began my annual chanting inside the bus, "Sack the sacks!" My group looked at me with odd expressions. Clearly, I am a diehard olive guy. From the farm, we followed the farmers to the mill we typically used for most of our production. In this instance, it was a local cooperative mill owned by the member farmers who utilize it annually to process their individual bounties. But the mills were not exclusive to great quality fruit. In fact, most of the fruit was very low quality. And often, the farmers sold their oil to brokers and bottlers who would ship that oil to Italy to be blended with many other oils to produce what we know on our shelves as "Mediterranean Blend" olive oil.

I had suggested to the founder that the mill should crush green olives during our visit, the olives that make Gaea oil. And as a harvest visit gift, we would bottle for each guest olive oil that had been freshly pressed in front of them, complete with their name stamped on it, and then have it shipped to their homes back in the US. What a treat, I thought! But given that we had seen the farmers picking purple fruit and transporting it in sacks, I was fearful of what olives might be crushed that day.

We watched the de-leafing process, which is always fun. The olives are dumped from the sad-sacks, already sweaty, and I feared, already fusty—a defect that is a result of the olives not having enough air moving around them (basically an anaerobic fermentation). I inquired of my boss if these were the olives that we would see being crushed and used to make Gaea. Again, he assured me they were not. I was relieved and started to keep an eye out for the bins of green olives waiting for our eager group. In the giant bins where the washed and de-leafed olives are held prior to crushing, I saw two separate groups of olives—black and purple over-ripe olives and green luscious-looking ones.

Black, overripe olives in Greece (Sitia), low-quality

Clearly, those were the Gaea olives. And I made sure to point this out.

With the help of the Greek mill manager (who spoke no English), I took the group past the crushing machinery, through all of the elements of making the oil. At the very end, out of the centrifuge, came a yellowish olive oil. And there stood two well-meaning staffers from Gaea's Athens office, collecting the oil, freshly made, into 500-milliliter tins, each with a different guest's name on each. I ran over and tasted the oil—it certainly was *not* Gaea EVOO. It already had a distinctly defective aroma and taste.

I scrambled to the founder and asked him why they were bottling what was clearly not Gaea oil, and he relayed, "This is what the plant is running at the moment and what the guests are witnessing, and they won't know the difference." To say I was horrified is an understatement. I asked them to stop. And I quickly explained to them that the timing wasn't ideal, and the beautiful, green Gaea olives that were staged in the bins waiting were not ready to run. There was a backup of local farmers who needed their fruit crushed. I wish I could end by saying this was an uncommon experience. I was embarrassed. But it seems to most producers, olives are olives; the oil they make is what it is. And my dogmatic insistence of working quality fruit through the mill to impress my guests is just me being picky.

The takeaway for you is: if you care about what you buy and eat, being picky is a right, never to be dismissed by others. I stood my ground then. And always have. And at Gaea, I had a QC (quality control) consultant check shipments of the product I represented to US consumers for consistency and quality to our brand promise. If producers can try to fool someone like me, think how easy they must think it is to fool you.

Then there are the good guys. Giorgio Franci, a second-generation Tuscan olive farmer, master miller, master blender, and bottler of some of the very best EVOO in the world (*Flos Olei* Guide Top 500 Producers, Hall-of-Famer 2020, 100/100 score 2020, 2021).

Giorgio has evolved into one of my most significant idols. Based in Montenero, a small ancient hillside village near Grosetto in Southern Tuscany, his *frantoio* [mill], *Frantoio Franci*, is everything you would dream of and more if you are a devotee of fine olive oils, like me. The view driving up the cobblestone hills to his property still sends chills down my spine. It's

Author and Girorgio Franci at his mill in Tuscany

humble in size. They must work within the confines of the space their building allows. You are met out front by a beaming Giorgio personally, usually wearing a green lab coat with his name embroidered on the pocket. A sign with your name welcomes you as their esteemed guest. I would visit my friend Giorgio during my annual Lucini Italia harvest trip, where I would meet current and future producers, evaluate their early harvest oils, watch the crushing, and most importantly discuss quantity and pricing for the year ahead.

At Giorgio's mill, bins of the greenest olives you've ever seen are dumped from a small tractor, freshly picked, and enter a chute to be de-leafed and then washed. But in 99 percent of all the other mills, the fruit heads directly to the crushing. Here, a conveyor slowly creeps by, taking the olives past half a dozen older local women who are looking for olives with color— meaning riper, or less fruity. Or damaged fruit. Indeed, the large commercial producers have robots and electronic cameras to undertake this grading. But Giorgio is old-school. He learned from his father, who spoke no English but was such a presence, and who sadly passed away a few years ago, that every olive can add value to a batch of EVOO—or take away from it. The takeaway for me here was, perfection cannot be compromised. A great bottle of olive oil begins with great fruit.

He works mostly with his own fruit or that of the neighboring groves that meet his high expectations. And when he declares the harvest begins, they work night and day, picking quickly to ensure minimal damage to the fruit, and then storing the freshly made EVOO in Inox stainless steel tanks in his temperature-controlled tank room, all while the oil is protected with nitrogen.

Before a typical visit ended for me, a lunch next door at a village *trattoria* was expected. No menu needed. The table was waiting for us, loaded with bottles of his best Franci olive oils.

Lunch came out one platter at a time, each more spectacular than the last. Freshly made rustic bread for us to dip into the Franci EVOO. Charcuterie, bruschetta, perhaps some sort of hot meat entree, a small pasta. And desserts. Accompanied by bold Tuscan red wines. A 4,000-calorie end to an always memorable visit to see how one of the best EVOOs in the world is made.

So as you see from the stories of the two mills, not all olive oil is made the same, and there are continual issues of quality. I won't tell you that a bottle of Franci is inexpensive, but if you believe that food actually feeds your soul, I can attest that this product delivers health and love. You can find a bottle of Franci in the US at specialty stores like Eataly in Los Angeles, Chicago, or NYC, or online (see the reference section). You may not be at his mill, but once you taste the production of his oil, you will recall this story and can experience a connection through sensorial excitement. Perhaps you are fortunate enough to have visited an olive mill, and if you haven't been to a really great mill yet, this oil will help you imagine what that visit might be like. It's an experience everyone should try to have at least once. They are my chosen family, and in many ways, I feel more connected to them than my own blood. Building relationships like these takes time, but I was open to learning how to integrate into their culture, while still maintaining my uniqueness.

One great example was a weekend trip to the Italian mountains with one of my producers at Lucini. As president and partner of Lucini Italia, I typically spent my visits with this family accompanied by my Italian sales and procurement office team—both for moral support and translations. But this group, as well-intentioned as they were, also kept a barrier between the producers and me. A real estate agent doesn't want their buying client to meet with sellers alone, nor did my Italian office want me to spend time alone with my producing partners. However, at one dinner, the daughter of the producing family made me an offer to spend a weekend on my next visit to Italy with her and her husband, alone for a weekend as their guest at a famous sulfuric spring. This, of course, worried me. I wasn't sure if they had an ulterior motive, which would be reeling me into their cultural Italian web of influence and saying, "If we take care of you, and you love us, you won't fire us." I would not be swayed by such actions. I was too committed to olive oil. And neither spoke English well. Months went by and I indeed returned to Italy for my usual visit. This time, I found time in my schedule for the weekend with this couple. Again, I knew I'd have wonderful meals and experiences with this pair, but business is business. I would not overlook the challenges over quality and price with them. I suspected this weekend was meant to try to lower the barriers that may have existed. I needed to keep my friends close and while it sounds extreme, my enemies closer.

The long journey in the car was curious. Hard to speak with each other. Hard to use hand gestures. But after hours of twisty, turning roads, we arrived at an amazing resort. I was shown my room and dressed for dinner. We enjoyed a gourmet meal and some wine, discussing both life and business. After a good night's rest, we awoke to meet for a long mountain walk and then changed into our swimwear for the reason they brought me there—the sulfur springs. Needless to say, it was relaxing. We did bond. There were exaltations of new projects, improvements desired on my side, a sharing of ideology. And most of all, common respect and appreciation for the work we all did. Without us, their business was very small. Without them, we wouldn't have had the volume of quality oil to sell that we did. This turned out to be much-needed time between colleagues, a customer and his clients, friends, and now family.

Family looks after each other. Family wants the best for each other. Family makes time to spend together. Family respects each other. Culturally, you are in or out. To be in means you may be cheated less often and able to push them harder on quality and price. If you are out, there will always be tension between parties. So in the interest of securing the best product and business terms, I allowed myself to get close—like family—to them.

The art of the producer (their special EVOO) leaves the mill and begins the long process of entering the US market, and into the stores. Now the stores are the gallery for this art. The quality of the presentation (shelf placement), the freshness of the product (rotating products), and promotions, which allow for visibility and trial, are all essential to completing the journey to "Ultra-Premium" or "Extra" extra virgin olive oil. The closer the relationship is between all the primary parties, the stronger the delivery of excellence.

We will get into the chain of supply, but first, let's make sure that as a smart and savvy consumer, you understand exactly what the EVOO is in the bottle you just bought.

EVOO FAST FACTS:

Unlike wine, where most producers/brands utilize similarly shaped bottles but have unique labels, better quality olive oil producers love to differentiate their oils by bottling their product in either custom molded glass bottles or traditional olive oil bottles, using either beautiful labels or etched onto painted glass. While I encourage you to appreciate the various designs, remember you are seeking great EVOO, not just a pretty bottle. Many olive oils will try to confuse a shopper with a fancy bottle, but the oil is still very low quality.

CHAPTER FOUR

What is EVOO really?

E xtra virgin olive oil is a relatively new agricultural product in the US, mainly because we didn't grow up with it. In Europe, extra virgin olive oil has been a dietary staple for thousands of years. Yet, US household consumption has gone up from 30 percent five years ago to 50 percent today. So more and more American consumers are buying olive oil, but the issue is that they don't know what they are buying, and they assume that a "real" bottle of EVOO—produced thousands of miles away, often from a family estate, with the fruit picked by hand, properly milled, stored, then shipped with nitrogen to protect the oil integrity—is too expensive. Not buying a good bottle of olive oil is cheating yourself and your household members from one of the simplest and most delicious daily compliments to your palate. A way to nourish your bodies and souls. Cooking with quality products is centering. It allows us to realize that we are independent and can utilize our sound judgment and minimal skills to produce a finished meal that satisfies our need for a balanced meal *and* tantalizes our palates.

Having been in the food industry my whole career, over thirty-seven years, I can say with confidence that a majority of consumers just want to take the easy path when it comes to their groceries. I am not saying this applies to you because you clearly have picked up this book to learn more about olive oil, but let's assume for a second that like millions of other Americans, shopping for you has become a weekly chore. Driven by a need to fill the cupboard and fridge for the next week, checking things off the list and settling for mediocre products, because any particular market is on the way home. This is not how most of the rest of the world shops. They market. They purchase food for the day, not the week. They buy local and seasonal and don't necessarily need to eat fresh peaches year-round. They do not have to think about whether food is properly sourced or not because they are at the source. If you are in California, you have the advantage of knowing more about your producers, but if you are in Alabama or North Dakota, not so much. Either way, because we don't shop daily, we have become apathetic to quality and food with soul.

To truly get the value to the dollar of what you are buying, you will have to make a more informed choice. I can assure you, once you do the investigation and make the list of what olive oils to buy, you will not feel hassled or turn back to junky

EVOOs. Plus, your food will be delicious. To get you to that place, I need you to understand the time and toil put into making a good olive oil and the egregious acts around horrible oil that are disguised as EVOO grade.

Life for most, if not all, of us has been challenging during the COVID-19 crisis of 2020 (and beyond). So many changes and limitations—in particular, the ease with which we used to dine out at local eateries we enjoyed and for some, traveling to exotic far-away lands like France, Greece, and Italy. Without those experiences readily available, we resorted to cooking from home, which I have seen as a blessing during the pandemic. Old cookbooks were opened, and we dove into the depths of long-forgotten spice shelves, asking, "When did I buy those bay leaves?" I chose to take it to the next level and watch all the old episodes of Julia Child and Jacques Pépin in *Cooking at Home*, the award-winning PBS series. Along with Julia and Jacques, I concocted versions of their dishes and was impressed with my cooking skills, which I had feared had gone rusty.

My wife Semone was, and still is, a busy executive. She never took the time or had access to trusted information to learn about olive oil. She just knew she liked it and was told to use it. When I first started dating her in 2014, I visited her home kitchen. My modus operandi is always to open the pantry in any house I visit and check their olive oil situation. The worst place I can find a bottle (or even worse a decanter/cruet) is by the stove. Heat is the #1 criminal of quality and is guaranteed to ruin your olive oil in days if it wasn't already rancid before. I found a bottle in her kitchen cabinet from a national natural grocer. Their private label offering stated "Italian oil." While the "best before date" hadn't been met, that date isn't trustworthy on any bottle, and it only applies to a bottle prior to being opened.

I knew before I unscrewed the top of what I would find. I mentally prepared myself. The smell hit me immediately. It was classified to me as *"Lampante"* (lamp oil). Clearly defective and a legally defined quality grade unfit for human consumption. She protested that she used it sparingly due to travel, and she claimed to have had it "hanging around" for months. I would have suggested a year. When she smelled and tasted my brand, which I had brought with me for the weekend visit, the alarm bells rang in her head, and I could see the expression on her face.

"Is this what real extra virgin olive oil is supposed to smell and taste like?" she asked.

Fast forward two years and her doctor ran the usual annual blood workup on her. She was startled with the results and inquired of Semone about what she had changed in her life. That was simple: a new man (me), increased yoga practice, and consuming "real" extra virgin olive oil daily (even multiple times a day!).

The doctor responded, "Well, I hope you are prepared to live forever because your blood work has vastly improved, and you have the blood chemistry of someone in their twenties, not their fifties!" Not everyone may have the same resounding results. But I saw firsthand how a commitment to use quality oil can positively impact someone.

The lesson here, which you will read repeatedly from me in this book, is to trust yourself once you have the basic knowledge I will teach you. Understanding, learning how to properly buy, taste, and serve extra virgin olive oil (EVOO) can bring you great peace of mind as a provider of food to yourself and your loved ones. Plus, with this new knowledge, you can be an expert to enlighten others.

Olive oil, as 99 percent of the US public knows it, isn't what it really is. In fact, *olive oil*, the term, is a generic reference. The USDA classifies olive oil in two distinct ways: unrefined virgin olive oil and refined olive oil. The refining process is widely used to repurpose olive oil that had quality issues or was produced from olives that were picked and crushed later in the harvest (overripe) and wouldn't be good enough to meet the extra virgin grade.

Unrefined is the more preferred production method if a consumer desires the benefits of what olive oils are purported to deliver—taste and health benefits. And it must result from the first cold pressing of the olives by mechanical means. All unrefined virgin olive oil can be graded "Extra Virgin," and the best quality in this category, but must not have any detectable sensory defects and the chemical analysis must also confirm the parameters. Refined olive oil is a product that should *not* be consumed raw, and its only real use from my perspective is for high-heat cooking where you don't want to spend money on a quality EVOO, and taste isn't a factor. The oil can be sold filtered (clear of all sediment) or unfiltered.

Some producers and brands believe in bottling unfiltered oil as is, or as "classic," and that it provides more flavor and/or health benefits. *This is false!* I strongly urge you not to purchase unfiltered olive oil. It is the Cheez Whiz of olive oil. You can find this product in all major supermarkets and often in the olive oil stores that retail bulk oil to the consumer. It was probably very good the day it was made. And if bottled fresh, will last usually ninety days. After that, it is most certainly rancid or could have a further defect called muddy sediment, a foul-smelling and tasting oil that no one will appreciate.

"Extra Virgin" is the highest grade of virgin olive oil, and this final product must meet stringent chemical and organoleptic analyses to have made that grade and include it on the label or documents accompanying that oil. This goes for when the oil is first made as well as when it is sold by the "best before date" on the bottle. This includes zero sensory defects, which must be determined by qualified panel tasters trained to find them. Sensory defects are half of the grading equation, and I devote an entire chapter (Chapter Seven) to defects. If defects are found organoleptically and/or via chemical testing, the oil could be decreased to grade "Virgin." However, you will never find virgin olive oil, labeled as such, in a bottle on a store shelf. Because the consumer doesn't know what that is, a bottler/brand wouldn't try to sell it. So while much of the olive oil on the shelf *is* actually virgin grade (slight defects detected) it is labeled as "Extra Virgin." Therein lies the fraud, be it intentional or unintentional. If the product is even worse than virgin, it would be *lampante*.

Despite knowing all of this new information, many bottle labels lie to you. Until you learn to taste, which I have simplified as a process and will teach you in this book, you should lean toward price as a quality indicator.

Over three million metric tons of olive oil is produced every harvest, globally. The majority of it originates from the EU (European Union) around the Mediterranean basin. Spain, Italy, and Greece have been the big three producers for decades. Now,

Tunisia and Turkey are adding to the annual numbers. Ethical producers who recognize they have olive oil that won't make the grade of extra virgin, and which would have earned them the most money per kilo available, ship their oils to a refinery where they are cleaned up and become refined oils, like Pure and Light. However, "Pure" olive oil actually means "purified" (a.k.a., fixed). Refined. Chemically produced. The oil started out at some point being made from olives, but they were likely defective or the oil was made as a secondary use of the pumice—the thick, brown, smelly sludge, which is a byproduct of making olive oil. Light olive oil actually means "light" in taste, as in, there is none. It does not mean light in calories. *All* olive oil contains the same caloric load: 120 calories per serving. These oils, however, have no taste, no aroma, minimal health benefits, and are produced in a non-natural process utilizing chemicals like Hexane as solvents. The olives establish their future grade as early as the bearing of fruit on the tree.

The United States is the single largest importer of olive oil in the world. Four-hundred thousand metric tons in 2020 and the producing countries that see the US as an eager business for their product, often dump their lowest quality oils on our shores, which would be illegal in most cases back in their home countries. The US only produces 5 percent of the annual consumption in America. Therefore, 95 percent of our olive oil needs will be satisfied by imported oil. That is why our shelves are full of low-quality oils. The producers cannot sell their low-quality oils easily, and in some cases, at all, in their countries of production, so they ship it to the US where we are less informed and think of olive oil perhaps like we do soy sauce.

The term *quality* can be misunderstood, especially when it comes to olive oil. Because, in part, olive oil is both very complicated to produce *and* even harder to maintain the original quality from the moment when the olives are crushed to finished oil reaches your table, as I explained in the previous chapter about where olive oil comes from. I'd say most producers have a QA (quality assurance) team or system in place where they produce. This should ensure that the quality parameters that the particular brand has established for their products are maintained along the production chain, allowing for quality variances due to annual harvest changes. You would think, and moreover expect, that any legitimate producer would insist that the product they are making meet or exceed the legal standards (IOC oversees the production in the participating countries, like the EU where the big three producers are). With olive oil, having witnessed hundreds of mills where the annual crushing of the olives takes place, I can say that I have seen everything from very rudimentary QA standards to highly scrupulous practices utilizing the most expensive production equipment available. In my opinion, the better the equipment, the better the resultant olive oil is. But that said, if a value brand is focused on volume sales and low price, then they must establish a consistent quality parameter that maintains their output with little variance. Meaning not any better or worse than the specification. And if this is the case, how can they adapt to almost annual changes in harvest qualities? And oftentimes, when I taste the oil, I discover defects that could only happen to the olives during the harvesting, crushing, or storage phases, not a result of lengthy transport or time sitting on a shelf. How can these oils still be bottled and labeled as

EVOO grade by their quality teams if they have tested the oils in their laboratories or sent them out to qualified labs and tasting panels? If the results return as having a defect—be it chemical or organoleptic—then these oils should never be sold as EVOO grade. That is unfair to both the properly labeled brands and the consumers. Yet, it does happen. A lot. In fact, in many countries, defective olive oil is preferred by their domestic consumers. Those people grew up with defective olive oil and developed a taste for it. So perhaps for producers, bottling a defective oil isn't as bad a practice as we may think. Except for one small detail—if they are selling this oil with a label that states the legal grade as "Extra Virgin," the choice is not theirs to make to defy the standards. Sadly, too many olive oil producers make oil that will sell cheaply. That is what the biggest part of the global market demands. So they become branded as a price-oriented producer. And with low price will come low quality. You cannot make a Mercedes for the price of a Hyundai.

The grocery store, where I suspect most US consumers shop for their olive oil, typically merchandizes these products in the baking aisle of the store. Unlike the full-service departments or even the produce section, the center of the store, as it is referred to, is a collection of thousands, even tens of thousands, of shelf-stable foods, ingredients, and other essentials. While olive oil and extra virgin olive oils can be used for baking, they are a specialty item and deserve a unique area, where preferably a staffer is available to answer questions. But sadly, this never happens. So when you are shopping for EVOO, head to the aisle, and you will find the likes of Crisco, Peanut, and Canola oils, even lard, another reason as a buyer you need to use extra care when shopping for a quality and authentic extra virgin olive oil.

If you are at the point of sale and you decide to check the back of the bottle before you purchase it and look for a "best before date" as a measurement of the quality or the life remaining of the product, the "best before date" cannot be trusted, as I stated earlier. It's a guide that producers use to add confidence to unwitting shoppers, and this is not required by the USDA to put on a label. And it only applies to unopened bottles. Typically, producers use two years from bottling (not harvest) as the "best before date." But rarely will a bottle last that long. So my recommendation is to disregard this date. The harvest date on the bottle, if available (since it isn't required), is far more reliable. You want to pick a bottle that has a harvest date if you can, and the year should be the most recent one. So if you are in the stores shopping in 2021, pass over a bottle with 2018, even 2019, and look for a harvest date of 2020. Many producers will actually include two years on their label, as their harvest can flow from one year to the next in the Northern Hemisphere (e.g., 2020/2021). This means their harvest started in the fall of 2020 but ended in the winter of 2021.

Then there is the term "First Cold Pressed," which is typically found on every bottle of virgin olive oils (natural/unrefined). We all know the term *virgin*, which means the first time. Well, olives that hope to be graded as virgin must be crushed once—their first time. If the oil is spectacular and meets all the criteria to be labeled "Extra Virgin," then that is the highest grade available. Generally, this means no heat exposure in the production phase above 72°F is used in the crushing and malaxation process. But this term was more relevant prior to the mechanization of olive oil when stone (granite) wheels and woven mats were used to crush and separate the oil from the paste. So this term contains little relevance to oils produced today. But if you asked any of your friends, "What kind of olive oil should I buy?" they would likely say two things: Buy Extra Virgin and buy First Cold Pressed. But if you asked them what either of these two indications meant, they probably couldn't answer that.

My exploration into the foibles of true, quality EVOO was when the brand Lucini Italia (Premium Tuscan Extra Virgin Olive Oil) was disqualified as *not* extra virgin grade from a start-up olive oil competition in 2013. I had requested the judges scoring notes to ascertain these results when we didn't even medal a silver, the lowest award. I was more shocked than anyone. How can this be? This was the grade we had claimed on our bottle for fifteen years and that consumers bought at the store in good faith. How could it *not* be extra virgin grade?

During the first five years as the president of Lucini Italia brand, Premium Tuscan Extra Virgin Olive Oil, I was encouraged by the founders to focus on sales, building distribution, and keeping our prices stable. We were already one of the most costly brands in the market. It wasn't possible to increase the quality of the Tuscan-made EVOO we purchased and had bottled for us in Italy. We were at the tipping point for the consumer. The red zone for EVOO pricing on the shelf is $20 for a 500 ml bottle. Over that price, sales drop to almost insignificant volumes. So it was imperative for me to discover what the problem was. This revelation forced me to the point where I had to ask more questions, to validate the quality that I was told met our contractual expectations with our producer.

I had not been trained in olive oil quality or sensory evaluation. I knew that to be in a position to drive change, I needed to expand my knowledge of olive oil. I attended the renowned *L'Organizzazione Nazionale Assaggiatori Olio d'Olivia* (ONAOO)—the first school to teach the official IOC method for tasting olive oil (since 1985) and who has trained over 15,000 students worldwide as a non-profit—for a week in Imperia, Italy. I felt I had to know more about what was in our bottles and didn't feel comfortable just taking the word of our founders or supply agents in Italy. I needed to have skills if I was to be trusted by our customers. (I later went on to attend their three-year, Level 2 Professional Taster program.)

Author graduating from the Level 1 Taster Class at ONAOO School, Italy

The one-week class, instructed in Italian with simultaneous interpretation in English, was certainly a challenge. And, as the only American in the class, I felt somewhat at a cultural disadvantage. But I ended up passing the exam, and I felt a world of improvement in my ability to smell and taste EVOO and understand qualities and defects. It was an ah-ha moment! Then a shoe dropped off one of my feet the next year.

At the first NYOO World competition in 2013, our Lucini EVOO entry was disqualified. A reality I wasn't prepared for. An eye-opener. But there was more to learn than just that my pricey oil didn't medal. In addition to the awards, I attended two days' worth of industry lectures. One speaker, whom I was most impressed with but didn't know personally, Alice Epstein, sold me ten olive oil defect wheels to better understand how flaws in EVOO can be identified. I bought them for myself, my staff, and a few select customers. I was able to get her business contact information and subsequently called her to ask about this competition and our lack of securing a medal. I was terrified of sharing our results with the founders. I'm not sure why since it was their oil and their source that produced the products we proudly sold. I inquired about what she did as an olive oil consultant and quality expert. Her resume was incredible. But did I need a resource like that? I had my quality and sourcing team in Italy. I had founders who were knowledgeable. In the end, I had the face-to-face meeting with the founders and suggested we retain Alice on a month-to-month retainer to allow her to help me discover what may have happened to our prized oil. To start, Alice and I tested more samples from inventory that we had in our US warehouses, ready to ship to stores, and discovered they were not holding up well (aging). Then we discovered that we perhaps had a bigger issue on our hands.

The summer of 2013 found me back in central Italy, a place I love to visit three to four times a year, but now I had Alice in tow. I was going to introduce her to our Italian team and then meet with our two suppliers, both in Tuscany but in very different areas. I was getting to the bottom of this issue of not meeting the quality criteria and knew she was the bird in the hand. Our first stop was Livorno, a majestic yet humble seaside port city, with all the Old-World charms many tourists would never discover because it isn't in the Top 10 Italian cities to visit lists. I would stay at the former residence of the former ruler of the city— which had since become a boutique hotel—The Grand Palazzo, next to the sea. A supremely romantic view to see every day.

On our first day and after the introductory grilling of the Italian sourcing team, we drove to the *frantoio* (mill) of one of our producers. The very one that had produced the lot of Lucini EVOO that didn't medal in New York and was disqualified for defects. This is a family I had grown very close to over the years. As our business scaled up, so did theirs. They had to continue to invest in equipment to meet our growth. I had watched them grow from a very small operation in 2006 to a formidable, premium crusher/bottler of quality EVOO in 2013. I had no reason not to believe they produced the very best olive oil. We all sat in the living room of their home.

They had invested in a translator to help ensure they didn't miss anything during our meeting. In the past, our Italian office staff had been sufficient. But given that I had brought Alice, and they had done their research on her, it was a good decision on their part. We chatted a bit about their sourcing of the olives that didn't grow on their estate, as well as any oil they purchased on our behalf to meet the needs of our annual production plan. I felt uneasy because these people all ensured me at every visit I made there and had been gracious, fun, and thoughtful. They would bestow magnums of fantastic, locally-made red wine to me. Every night was a major group dinner where the chef used my EVOO. Whatever they thought would be special for me, they wanted to do. It's impossible to say no. They take rejection very personally, so I was warned and trained early to be gracious. But it always made me uncomfortable. Maintaining an arm's length relationship in any business is wise. Especially in Italy where we're on their turf.

Finally, with all the players in the room, I had to make my concerns known. And I know our Italian team had already tipped them off. This became another awareness moment for me; Italians protect fellow Italians. It didn't matter that my team was paid by me to supervise them. Now, they became allies, seemingly against me. And I was left hanging in the wind. It was time to stand my ground. My one week of olive oil school versus their generations of experience and respect in the industry.

I shared with this family—with the proud father staring me down, the heartfelt daughter (and heir) looking at me with warm eyes, and the son-in-law ready to beat me up—that we had not taken a medal in the NY competition months earlier, that our sample was disqualified as "Rancid"—a legal defect that can affect even the best olive oils at any stage of the storage, bottling, shipping, warehousing, shelving, and home use. This means it was not recognized as EVOO grade, which is devastating to a brand like ours. The family happened to have handy a bottle with the same lot number as our failed bottle. We tasted it together. It tasted like our recipe. I darted my eyes to Alice for her "expert" opinion. She had not only been a panel leader in California for years, and supervised the official tasting panels that producers relied on to gain confirmation that their oils could be called EVOO, but was also the chief judge of a number of respected olive oil competitions. So her opinion mattered. Her conclusion on the sample they had was that it was "tired." The oil was "flabby." It may have been on the edge of rancid. But, the point was, it wouldn't make it to the shelf life stamped on every bottle—in this case, two years out. You could have heard a pin drop in that room. She was telling olive oil royalty, a multi-generational family known for producing some of the best olive oil in Italy, that their product was not excellent. And furthermore, was on the verge of going bad. I had a momentary fleeting thought, asking myself how much did I love the olive oil business? And maybe when I returned, I should think about cleaning up my resume. This meeting did not feel good.

After those few tense moments, I suggested we review our concrete supplier agreement, signed years earlier by all parties, and by which they had to contractually agree to various stipulations. These included but were not limited to: cultivars (types) of olives to be used in specific proportions to create the "Lucini LPS Blend;" the area in which these olives had to originate from (the Province of Tuscany only); and nitrogen had to be used in both the storage tanks where the olive oil was stored (in a climate-controlled building to prevent damage from heat) and in the head-space of every bottle after it was filled (as a replacement for air that if left in a bottle of oil creates oxidation and can lead to a very unstable product and shorten the shelf life, leading to rancidity). We began to probe the oil taste, via Alice's palate, and she picked up a taste that wasn't an olive cultivar that originated in Tuscany. Both our Italian team and the producers strongly defended their use of the classic four olive cultivars from the required region.

But when she pressed them and suggested she send the oil to a lab in Germany, EuroFins, for NIR (near-infrared testing) to determine the DNA footprint of the makeup of the olive fruit in the bottle, they begrudgingly admitted that the olive campaign of 2012 (October/November), which that lot number (and the bottle we sent to the competition for judging) originated from, actually had some Coratina variety olive oil blended in, came from Puglia. Southern Italy. Not Tuscany.

The family explained that they had run short of the cultivars we required in our contract but didn't disclose this nor even ask our permission. You can imagine my horror. I shot a look at the general manager of my supply-side team from Livorno. The very one who attended olive oil school with me a year earlier in Imperia. This alone could lead to an invalidation of our supply agreement with the producer. The room became hotter. I didn't like where this was going, but like a blood-draw, better to get it over with. We had come this far.

That alone was not the smoking gun we were looking for. Since neither my supply team nor the producing family would be transparent with me, we needed to dig deeper. We asked to go into the bottling line and watch firsthand how Lucini EVOO was bottled. This would be Alice's first time in their very secretive building. Trade secrets are revered in olive oil production.

We donned the required white jackets, hairnets, and shoe covers and started with the tank room where the oil was stored. Always an impressive sight. Giant stainless steel silos emanating from the concrete floor, climbing up over three stories to the gangway where we would view them and always take a ceremonial photo. They held hundreds of thousands of liters of not inexpensive extra virgin olive oil, waiting for orders. Then we moved to the filling and closure lines. Fully automated, also an impressive sight. The system married traditional quality with modern packaging processes.

But the all-important question came up: "Where is the nitrogen line (which is always blue tubing)?" I inquired. Where are the nitrogen bottles and on-site nitrogen generator? We didn't see any blue lines or large tanks that would hold nitrogen. I saw a look of surprise, then horror on the faces of our hosts. The son-in-law, whom I had grown to really like—even though he spoke no English and I spoke about five words of Italian—blurted out in something in Italian, and their translator turned it into English: "It's in the air." We all looked around.

"What does that mean—in the air?"

He reiterated, "Air is made up of a combination of gases, and nitrogen is one of them—78 percent, in fact, so when we clean the bottles before filling, we blow forced air into the bottles, which contains some nitrogen." And so came the much-needed answer to why the fantastic Lucini olive oil was not holding up well. A pivotal moment in my career.

Finally, after months of pondering, reading the judges' notes at the NY competition, hiring Alice, tasting many samples, and grilling our supply team in Italy, we had our answer. The oil wasn't stable because they had changed the formulation, *and* they never used nitrogen in the bottles, which is one of the best and only ways a producer can protect against aging and possible rancidity through oxidative stress. Both were major violations of our supply agreement. Both were untenable. I felt misled and more than that, totally taken advantage of . . . because I was a dumb American who didn't really know what olive oil should taste like. Well, it turns out that I did know a little and had the authority to make changes, and this dumb American invalidated the supply agreement for the remainder of the production year until such a time as the producers could prove they met the contractual criteria, which they did later that year after they made a major investment in their facilities. That cost them plenty of sales to me. Plus the costs to purchase and install a nitrogen line were large.

But for you, the reader, this highlights the intense reality that even as the president of a well-respected brand, loved by Oprah, who had sold in the market for fifteen years by that time . . . even I could be misled, and the quality could be changed without my knowledge.

Extra virgin olive oil is a food filled with a mired history, both pleasure and pain, and is revered in most of the world, even in some unlikely places, like Japan. It fascinated me from my first day in the industry back in 2006. And I have continued working with this magical, wonderful food ever since. I make people smile when I expose them to beautiful EVOO. And it is time for you to start smiling too. But there is more to learn before you are fully ready to take on the chore of accepting only *good* olive oil in your house or at your restaurant table. And really good oil—the stuff that will make you smile, isn't cheap.

EVOO FAST FACTS:

There are over 1000 cultivars worldwide that are known to be used to make olive oil. Each country has its own, based on what originated on that particular land. In many cases, olive trees have been transported to faraway lands, where they were not indigenous. I have had terrific Hojiblanca, a Spanish cultivar made in Australia, or a Frantoio cultivar from Tuscany grown in Cape Town, South Africa. Be open to them all. You get to decide what you like best.

CHAPTER FIVE

What Should I Spend?

So in this quest to consume real, and the best extra virgin olive oil within your budget, I must educate you on the facts of olive oil pricing. The best question to the olive oil riddle isn't why the good stuff is more expensive, but rather why the bad stuff can be purchased so cheaply. I can assure you, for the latter, the reasons are not acceptable to your palate or for your family's table.

Price is one of the arbiters of quality, which I agree is one way to establish a quality positioning. If you wanted to buy champagne for a celebration, a $7 bottle and a $100 bottle are fundamentally different in quality. When you pay *over* $10 for a bottle (17 oz, 500 ml) of extra virgin olive oil, it's more likely that the product will meet the grade as labeled, providing there haven't been damage-causing, disqualifying defects. For better brands, expect to pay closer to $18–$20 a bottle. You may call it "expensive," but that word is relative. The truth is, the cheaper olive oil is *too inexpensive*, and there are a variety of reasons as to why. The old tried and true phrase: "You get what you pay for" holds true with EVOO.

One of the most popular elements of the hundreds of Olive Oil 101 classes I have instructed has been a specific slide I show to the students with a comparable group of products, including those many of us buy regularly. Lipstick at Walgreens, for example, is $13.50 for a 0.16 oz tube (a cursory search on the web of what it costs to make a tube of a popular brand of lipstick is $1). A Starbucks latte is $5.49, which is consumed in thirty minutes or less also costs about $1 to make. A trendy, fresh-pressed "green" juice or Kombucha drink can be upwards of $11 for a few gulps and would likely cost the manufacturer $2 to produce using fresh ingredients. We don't even bat an eye at the price tag on these items. Yet, consumers seem to think extra virgin olive oil should be $7.99 or less for a 17 oz bottle. They are almost shocked when they are asked to spend $13 for a bottle. There are thirty-three servings in that bottle. That works out to $.24/per serving!

A $7.99 bottle of olive oil costs the producers about $2 to make, using the same model as the above products and their markups. We are dealing with an issue of an incredible decrease in the quality of that oil. If anyone believes they are receiving acceptable quality and flavor with health benefits for a production cost of $2, they are incorrect. If I suggested that really good

EVOO, full of flavor, with all the positive attributes you would expect from a well-made oil, with a solid level of polyphenols (and other measurable health benefits)—and that you can use less of because it is far more fruity than the typical supermarket brands—was twice as much in price on the shelf ($15.99 for the same 17 oz and thirty-three servings, and the per-serving price is now $.48/per serving) would you still declare this "expensive?"

Producers that are making the high-end olive oil are often wealthy and subsidize the cost of growing, harvesting, and making their product, which is how they can deliver a great oil even for $20 retail a bottle. That price has all the importing, warehousing, and up-charging from the wholesalers' and retailers' profit margins included. In the Trump retaliatory tariff of 2020 (Airbus WTO settlement), Spanish olive oil—all grades— were taxed an additional 25 percent to be imported into the US, except for large bulk containers used for re-packaging or blending. Every Spanish producer of quality I know ate that tariff in order to maintain stable retail prices. They are going into their pockets because they have a passion to bring top-quality extra virgin olive oil to our marketplace and not add another layer of possible discourse by the consumer. Their price is exactly what it should be—and it is *not* expensive.

I helped you understand what it actually takes to make a bottle of great olive oil in Chapter Three. And conversely, if a great bottle costs twice what a typical grocery store product is priced at, the crappy EVOO prices are driven down through lower quality fruit, more efficient land management (pruning, spraying, irrigation), more mature fruit that yields higher quantity but lower quality, as well as a lower cost of harvesting, less emphasis on quality manufacturing, no inert gas to protect the oil in the storage silos, and even the use of in-house blown PET plastic bottles to sell the oil in. There is always a trade-off when it comes to food production and quality.

Olive oil is labeled a "commodity" for agricultural purposes so pricing isn't arbitrary. Much of the olive crop is farmed and then sold to millers who produce the oil, then sell to bottlers or sell it in bulk for further packaging, such as in large tins for restaurants. The grade "Extra Virgin," the highest grade, which I have written mostly about so far, also has a global spot price by which commercial buyers can gauge a market price.

Pool Red is the spot price for olive oil that is managed globally and represents the lowest quality of extra virgin by determining the lowest price. Extra virgin can also mean the absolute lowest quality possible to legally meet that grade. Harvest forecasts and oil reserves carry over from one harvest year to the next, affecting price indexing and other metrics. The people I work with don't base their pricing on that base number, but it remains a respected guidepost for pricing of a typical quality (the lowest and still legally EVOO grade). As of the harvest of November 2020, the going bulk price for a typical EVOO was $2.99 a liter. A liter is two x 500 ml (17 oz) bottles, the most popular size for a US consumer. That equals $1.50 a bottle (17 oz) worth of the oil at cost. And that is before the other production costs—transport to the bottling plant, storage, bottling overhead, packaging materials, outer case packing, the pallet, and profit for the bottler. So what quality do you think the multinational bottlers are providing? Quality isn't expensive, it's priceless.

The bottlers who own their own land and trees, such as Giorgio Franci, will have very different costs for their oils. They typically don't buy olives to crush or buy oil to bottle. They are less affected by market swings. Of course, they have their overhead and their crops can be negatively affected just the same. But they have a bigger view of the market and accept that changing prices every year can be a death sentence to their own brand or one they may pack for. These are proud farmers who revere the land and the olive trees and thus cultivate and harvest olive fruit before it is ripe, where a higher return can be achieved due to higher quality fruit than a later harvest can yield. These noble landowners believe that making great EVOO is a life's work, and they take enormous pride in their finished products. I will teach you how to recognize a product like this as you read this book. And once you become passionate about this mysterious food, you will never go back to the standard bottles again.

On the other side of the industry are the large multinational bottlers, who are well known for the volume of products they sell in almost all points of sale in US stores. They purchase their oils in bulk, often from multiple countries, and then blend it. If they have $2 a bottle of total costs into each bottle, that's a good working number for a consumer to consider when they understand the other costs of getting bottles to the shelf (which we will discuss later).

As a professional in this industry, when I see a grocery store olive oil that retails for less than the global spot price for the oil alone, forget the bottling, shipping, and profit margins along the way, I can see that something funny is happening. And by funny, I don't mean "haha." I mean likely rancid oil is on the shelf. As a retail consumer, your best bet to gain better choices in a good bottle of EVOO is to expect to pay far more than any grocery store major brand. If you don't, at least my book will tell you the truth about what you are buying, and you need to live with what's on your table.

Because "real" EVOO, which has been properly graded as such, has a standard of excellence that must be met to carry that grade on its label, there is a cost associated with that quality. But all too often, I will try a bottle of the give-away price, and it fails to meet the criteria for EVOO grade that I have been trained to know well. It's not my role to point out this deficiency to the retailer who decided to sell and promote it, nor to the producer. But just know these pricing games exist, and you may have fallen prey to them. As the shelf price goes up, so too will the quality correspondingly. And with that pricing increase, you may become less and less familiar with the brand names.

This is typical with many consumer brands. Don't shy away from higher-priced EVOO or a brand you don't hear spoken about. This may be the bottle you have always thought about trying but just never had the courage or reason to reach for it. So let me break it down for you in layman's terms. To purchase "real" EVOO, not something that was EVOO and degraded, you will have to be willing to pay more than the bare minimum price. Again, just remember the tried and true saying: You get what you pay for. If you want a store brand of olive oil, don't expect too much. If you want to pay as little as possible, the oil will be worth every penny . . . but not a penny more. The higher the price, the better the oil and likely the better the producer, and your chances of starting with a product that will retain its excellent properties is better than a bottle that you buy for $6 for 17 oz in a PET plastic bottle.

I am in no way trying to make it sound elitist when I speak about considering a higher price for EVOO. I have explained there is a direct correlation between price and quality. A $6 bottle of olive oil and a $16 bottle, both the same size, will be very different products. Much like hamburger and filet mignon are very different products. Most of us like both cuts of meat. When we just need something quick, we eat a hamburger. When we prefer a more elegant meal with better quality, we would defer to a filet. (Those who eat meat, of course). The point of the metaphor is, don't expect filet mignon quality for hamburger price. It is the same with EVOO. And that $16-plus bottle will last you. In fact, a producer of consumer wine accessories launched a bottle of Argon gas for wine enthusiasts to protect the wine once the bottle is opened. A Silvadore wine preserver holds enough Argon gas (completely inert—no taste or smell) to protect thirty bottles of wine. When used with EVOO, it will also greatly reduce the oxidation of your oil once the bottle is opened. So if you are a slower user or travel, this small investment will lengthen the life of your bottle.

When you finally get past this barrier of price and change your EVOO choices, you will truly learn to cherish the oil that was born from olives that were tended to by people who love their land and love their work. To them, making an oil you savor isn't just a job. Or a penance. It's their passion. It's their livelihood. And accepting this will release your inner desires to enhance your diet with one of the original foods humans ate. A life force that hasn't changed much in 4,000 years. Then paying the price that is *fair*—don't think of it as expensive—will be easy for you. And you will have reached the end of paying too little and getting too little for your money.

So go to your cupboard. What do you have in there for olive oil? If it is a low-quality brand, discard it. I am sure it has long gone bad. Next, let me equip you with a cheat sheet you can bring to the grocery store to ensure you bring home the right EVOO choice.

EVOO FAST FACTS:

A typical olive tree that produces olives to make olive oil, harvested early in the annual campaign, usually yields five liters of olive oil. That's only ten typically-sized bottles (17 oz), all for a year of work to maintain that tree and then harvest its fruit. Think about the time and investment made by the farmer. So now is a bottle of great oil worth $20 to you?

EVOO Shopping Cheat Sheet

When you go to a meat case and shop for a steak, if that steak is dark/off-color and doesn't look as fresh as the rest, would you buy it? If not, why not? Could it be bad?

Meat Case: Notice the discolored steak?
Used with permission by Mary Franco

What if the butcher offered it to you for 50 percent off, would you buy it? And would a credible, integrity-based meat manager allow a dark, obviously spoiled cut of meat be displayed and sold like this? If your answer is no, you don't want it, even at a discount, then you do know something about meat. You don't have to be a professional butcher to know this.

This same metaphor holds true for fresh fish, produce, even deli products. You can't tell from looking in a bottle of olive oil what is in it. So that is why even a smidge of basic know-how about olive oil is helpful in your arsenal of food shopping skills.

- Price is a realistic criterion so the more you are willing to pay, the better the quality you'll get. Retail prices vary greatly by chain/store, but a good working range for a decent bottle of EVOO—not on sale—should be a low of $10 for an 8 oz bottle/250 ml (which equals $40/liter) or $17+ for a bottle of 17 oz/500 ml ($34/liter).

- Look for a single country of production. "Product of Spain" or "Product of Italy," as examples. There are at least a dozen great producing countries. But avoid any bottle that states, "Imported from . . ." That means it was also bottled in the country where it declares it was imported from and is always a blend of various oils from various countries. The back of the label must, by law, declare where the oil possibly originated. So you will see, in that case, "May contain olives or olive oil from XXX, or XXX, or XXX." And usually, the countries' names are abbreviated, such as IT for Italy, SP for Spain, TU for Tunisia, and MO for Morocco.

- If the label provides a harvest year, that is a great sign of potential quality. Only the better producers are brave enough to list the harvest year (or period). And the year may cover two years, as I mentioned earlier.
- If acidity is listed, this is another tell-tale sign of a quality oil. The legal limit for free fatty acids (FFA) in extra-virgin-grade olive oil is 0.8. The lower the number, the better the oil.
- Other indicators of quality that you should look for on the bottle are: hand-picked, crushed within a few hours, bottle-packed with inert gas to protect quality (nitrogen or argon), estate-grown, or limited production. These are key words.
- A good, reputable producer will also help you with tasting direction to ensure you will like the intensity of its fruitiness. You'll notice descriptions, such as intense, medium fruity, or delicate. But be warned; some bigger national grocery store olive oils are starting to use these terms, which are meant to be a distraction for the novice.
- What you should *not* use as indicators of quality are marketing words, which include: organic, Kosher, non-GMO, imported, pure, light, mild taste, clear bottles, and a far-off "best before date." I have seen some products boast a three-year shelf life. That oil was probably bad from day one.

If you come upon a sale at a store or online of really great EVOO, perhaps even a brand you have come to love, buy a few of them. As long as you do not open them, they will last. Try to use your olive oil quickly. Only purchase the size of bottle that meets your needs. If you live alone, I suggest a smaller size, such as an 8 oz (250ml) bottle. For a family of two to four, I suggest a 17 oz (500 ml) bottle, and a larger family should consider a 25 oz (750 ml) or even a 33 oz (1 liter). Do the math. Each person should consume 30 ml a day. This includes eating out.

30 days x 30 ml = 900 ml or 1 liter per person per month. This is optimal but likely not popular.

Don't be afraid to use great olive oil a lot.

Know the oil you use, and use it liberally.

EVOOGuy

Now, go and do it.

CHAPTER SIX
Don't Be Duped

I f you don't know what you are buying, then you likely will
end up with a product that isn't what it is labeled to be,
may not come from where you think it did, may actually
be rancid and inedible, and be a waste of your valuable food
shopping dollars.

Olive oil is an erratically used product surrounded by mis-
information. This is not the case for someone who, say, grew up
in Greece, where olive oil is used in every meal—all day, every
day. They, though, will often eat defective olive oil because that
is what they have known for generations. But at least they are
clear in what they are receiving versus American consumers
who have the power of choice but don't know it. They are being

duped. We need to get your taste buds knowledgeable about good oil, and that is the most effective solution to this fraud.

We have been hypnotized for decades by many brands, to shop for price and convenience, not quality. Even high-profile doctors, like Dr. Gundry, espouses his seemingly tall tales and claims of long life when you use *his* Moroccan olive oil (which I believe is overpriced). There have been a lot of mixed signals sent to the consumers, which makes it hard for someone with good intentions to figure out what to purchase. Then you add label fraud (or duping) to the mix, and it is a consumer's worst nightmare.

There have been many changes to the industry over the last fifty years. Olive oil was made popular with Americans in the 1972 Francis Ford Coppola film, *The Godfather*, which is set in the 1920s, has the main character, Vito Corleone, operating an olive oil import business called Genco Pura Olive Oil Imports. He supplies the Italian immigrants of New York City with a product similar to what they were accustomed to consuming back home in southern Italy (specifically Sicily and Calabria). Moving away from stone crushing, pressing the olive paste on dirty mats to extract the oil, picking the olives earlier in the harvest to improve the quality of the oil, and transporting the olives in bins that allow air to pass over the fruit versus jute sacks, to crushing the olives within hours of their harvest versus days are just a few of these essential changes.

The US government has a voluntary labeling rule outlined in the Olive Oil Act of 2010, which producers are encouraged to utilize as a guide. It is intended to be followed and honored. This Act of the USDA is a set of well-intended guardrails meant for producers and bottlers to work within to ensure the consumer is getting what they pay for. But like anything, what is measured is met. No accountability to the US government and no penalties for unscrupulous producers equals problems for the consumer. I stated in Chapter Four that the US only produces 5 percent of the annual consumption. Of the 95 percent of the oil that is imported, approximately 90 percent originates in the Mediterranean regions, primarily Spain, Italy, and Greece. As well, Tunisia has become a very dominant exporter of olive oil to the US in recent years. All of these countries fall under the umbrella of regulation of the International Olive Council (IOC), based in Madrid, Spain.

The IOC was formed in the 1980s by the United Nations to harmonize olive oil standards around the world. However, three major olive oil-consuming countries do *not* recognize their oversight and regulations: Brazil, Australia, and the United States. This is for a number of reasons, but, in part, for the US, the IOC standards are considered too low for the USDA to accept. To put it another way, 95 percent of the olive oil the US imports must be produced to the IOC standards to be exported, but once it arrives, the USDA neither recognizes this nor has their own legal standard by which they oversee the accuracy of the product or label claims. Only the voluntary Olive Oil Act of 2010 exists as a standard that producers, bottlers, and importers are instructed to follow. In no way are these standards supervised by the US government, which opens the doors for mislabeled and possibly fraudulently labeled olive oils to make their way to store shelves and into consumers' carts. In fact, this initial voluntary standard parallels the IOC standards in many ways, and where they are aligned is in accepting zero sensory defects in Extra Virgin Grade oil. We will expand into defects in the next chapter. However, in a revised version of this standard in 2012, the USDA weakened its stance on bottled olive oil under their Quality Monitoring Program, which allows domestic bottlers of imported olive oil to claim the standard Extra Virgin on the product that was evaluated with sensory/organoleptic defects of a two out of ten intensity or less. This is a *big* dupe, considering the oils were likely produced in the EU or a country that is recognized by the IOC as one that disallows any sensory defects to be called Extra Virgin. Confused yet?

So I have accepted that the bigger exporters of olive oil into the US have little to no incentive to send over their best quality bulk olive oils to package for US consumers. That is reserved for sale in IOC-regulated countries, where violating the regulations is often a criminal offense. In fact, in Italy, there is a division of the Italian police, the *Carabinieri* and the *Guardia di Finanza*, who have been trained as olive oil tasters at the same school I attended. So when they pull over a tanker of olive oil headed for the port or a bottler, they can, with a swirl, smell, and taste, determine if they have a questionable product that may not meet the standards of the grade listed on the shipper's manifest. What I am saying is . . . they send over olive oil to us that most all other countries will not accept.

The issue of bottles that started out well-intentioned as EVOO grade and then declined to the point where they are no longer legally able to be sold as Extra Virgin at the point of sale, is a multi-generational problem. I call it mislabeling because the quality of the oil and the labels applied are the responsibility of the producer/bottler. Even if it starts as Extra Virgin at the point of production, the laws state that the product must maintain that grade on the front label (this is a claim)—known as the principal display panel (PDP)—until the expiry of the "best before date" printed on the unopened package. This is a legal packaging requirement of the FDA, which oversees label compliance. It is ironic because the FDA maintains labeling oversight but the USDA has a voluntary standard for meeting the grade claimed. The USDA is concerned with food safety, not oil quality supervision or labeling claims. The US is not auditing inbound shipments for a quality match—what the shipment really is versus what is on the manifest. In fact, Tunisia is the only exporting country that actually tests all outbound olive oil shipments to confirm the grade claimed on the label.

Many US importers look the other way and many grocery store buyers and chain quality assurance managers don't hold suppliers accountable. It is up to the individual producers to meet the standards the USDA has made public. Like driving the speed limit—you are only breaking the law for speeding if you get pulled over by the police. Typical olive oil, as a product, is a low-quality product and contains refined oil. This is very different from EVOO grade, which has the taste and health benefits consumers desire when consuming and cooking with a healthy oil. You will have to become a judge of quality to best determine if the olive oil you purchase or use at a restaurant is a low-quality oil or not. And what do you think the grade claimed is in 99 percent of the cases? You betcha. Extra Virgin.

Unless you, as the consumer, can tell the difference, you will continue to consume defective, mislabeled olive oil and support the very producers who bottle and ship their products to us.

You may ask, how can a producer be responsible for changes in quality and product degradation once it has left its point of origin? That's an excellent point. And one with a difficult answer.

Two sure ways of reducing the possibility of product quality change are: start with a higher quality product if you intend to make the highest level of the quality claim, EVOO. This ensures a better chance the oil will not degrade as quickly in route to your home. This includes bottling the oil in dark bottles to reduce the damage from light and capping all bottles or bulk drums with nitrogen or Argon gas to vastly reduce oxidation. The second, manage all the points of handling until it reaches the store to ensure as minimal damage to the product in transit as possible. Just like a milk producer has to maintain their product at very specific temperatures to ensure freshness and safety, so must an olive oil producer. They are both highly perishable but in different ways.

I don't see any real possibilities for change until the US government (USDA) does two vital things: adopt a standard of identity for olive oil (SOI)—which legally defines what the standards are—and then reinforce the grades claimed on the labels, as they do with terms like "organic," which the USDA began to regulate in October 2002 under the National Organic Program (NOP). This created, once and for all, a level playing field for all organic foods being sold in the US and provided consumers with trust in that claim so they could be sure they are getting what they pay for. The penalties for violating the NOP are severe: $10,000/day until rectified. Juice, as another example, has an SOI; therefore, any claims where the word "juice" is used on the label *must* meet strict guidelines, which eliminate consumer confusion.

One day, olive oil will too. Petitions were filed by separate interested parties to the USDA in 2019 and 2020 to request that olive oil be issued an SOI (standard of identity), a legal definition of what olive oil is, and listing relevant parameters of quality and measurements. Without this, olive oil is lingering with a lack of standards and government oversight. As of this writing, no action has been taken. So consumer confusion continues. Until then, as a consumer of EVOO, you are on your own. This is the lesson I had to learn for myself.

Olive oil is much more than just a condiment, and as we are using it more and more, we can't blindly trust the food store where we shop to make wise assortment decisions. Maybe you think restaurants wouldn't allow bad olive oil to be available to their valued diners? How about a Michelin-starred fine dining restaurant? Well, that's exactly what I thought in France in the summer of 2019. And not just once. The oil was inedible, defective to the point where no one should consume it. *Lampante.* Unfit for humans to eat. Oils like this have only two legitimate destinations: the oil refinery to be cleaned up and then correctly labeled as olive oil (a blend of refined and virgin oils) or made into soap. I warned the people I was traveling with not to use this oil on their food. Only one listened to me. The rest did what most Americans do, lavish their 100 € meal with it. What a waste of what could have been an amazing, memorable meal.

I imagine you don't know the questions to ask. Why would you? There is no one standing in the olive oil section at the supermarket to help you, and the information online is definitely questionable. So how do you judge what to do if you purchase bad olive oil or discover it at a restaurant? Picture this—standing in front of the array of olive oil bottles at a store in complete confusion. Bottles with images of peasants picking the olives. Fancy terms splattered all over the labels. They sure look real, and you think: why would they lie? Can they lie?

Absolutely! Italian-sounding brands that say the oil comes from Tunisia? Guess again. Bottles that look great but the oil inside may be worthless? You bet!

Many brands contain oils produced in Spain, Morocco, Tunisia, Portugal, Greece, Italy, or even Cypress. Some brands buy these bulk oils and ship them to the US to be bottled. By US law, the product *must* list where the product originates from (e.g., Imported from Italy doesn't mean a product of Italy). Product of Italy means that oil would only have been produced with Italian olives. Consumers don't know what to buy. So how can you overcome these challenges in the olive oil section? Look for a single country of origin and don't buy on price alone. Open it when you get home, if it doesn't smell and taste wonderful, put the top on it, and take it back to the store . . . tell them it is no good. Don't say it is bad, or you don't like it. That could hinder your ability to return it. I ran gourmet food stores for seven years. I know how customer service will usually respond. With a receipt, you can expect your money back. Without a receipt, you'll usually get a store credit. Buy something else and start again. In Chapter Ten, I will teach you some basic smelling and tasting skills that will empower you to become a better EVOO shopper and a confident "at-home taster."

I explained that the value of oil can be initially determined by the price point in Chapter Five, and now, we add to your education by understanding what it really means when the labels say REAL "Extra Virgin Olive Oil." I want you as a shopper to see through the marketing magic on labels by understanding the differences between all the terms we see when we shop. Yes, I just said magic because that is the truth of what is being done by many producers. For example, let's consider bottled water. Do you want purified water or spring water? What is the difference? Does water have to travel from say, Fiji, to be good? Can I just use any water? I am not a water expert, but I am an olive oil expert. And expert opinion and knowledge are what you will get as you turn these pages. Know this: Olive oil is the single most tampered with food in the world.

When I use a term like "fraud," I do not write this lightly. The word *fraud* according to the revised and updated version of the Random House Webster's Dictionary is: "deceit or trickery." Because the harvesting, crushing, storage, and bottling of olive oil has many variables, and add to that, the shipping of oils on cargo ships takes weeks, even months, where the product is exposed to extreme heat, and the oils suffer. With most Americans placing little value on the fluid, to begin with, low price drives down the impetus for producers to take the best care they can with their olive oils. Hence, what seems like a good deal at the store or online, is very likely olive oil that was either knowingly packed with a poor quality product that didn't meet the legal standards to declare the grade on the label, or acceptable oil was bottled or containerized and because of the conditions of transport and later storage, changed grades and no longer met the standards claimed. Either way, fraud was committed.

It is the responsibility of the bottler, be it their own brand name or a private-label brand they bottle for, to achieve basic practices. Most important is food safety and truth in labeling. Producers get away with bottling bad oil, or oil that is at the very end of the quality spectrum because of the three-plus million metric tons of olive oil produced in the world, very little of it meets the Extra Virgin, highest grade standard. Yet this is the grade consumers desire most and the one which commands the highest price per kilo. So some producers bottle a product they believe is Extra Virgin. It does need to be tested to verify this. The results are called COA (certificate of analysis). They typically accompany a shipment of products to the importer of record. But many of these tests are handled with internal labs and tasting panels. Not objective third-party organizations. I always suggest to retail buyers that they require a COA from every brand of EVOO they sell that *only* originated at an IOC accredited third-party lab and panel.

The retail buyers do look at their assortment annually. This is called a "review." They consider new product submissions, line extensions of existing brands, weed out slow sellers, and look for trends to incorporate into their sets (shelving layouts). With a few exceptions, I have not found many buyers who actually care about the fluid in the bottle. And so the cycle of deceit continues.

I have also been an advocate for producers to properly label their oils. I wish producers would help educate the US market on the benefits of using virgin olive oil and offering support for farmers and producers who have oil that had an issue, and they don't wish it to be sold for the lowest price and head to the refinery.

In fact, when I was CEO at Gaea North America, I did launch a first-of-its-kind branded virgin olive oil. A lower price than our extra virgin. It was meant to help the farmers but the market was not ready to fracture. There is not enough extra virgin olive oil in the market. People are being sold false EVOO. I was trying to bring truth to the shelf. I spent a lot of time and company resources to educate people on why we felt this was useful in the market. After a disappointing first year, we didn't continue selling this item. The grocery stores would not get behind it, and consumers did not know what to do with virgin olive oil. They still wanted to believe they were being sold the best, even though they weren't, and were reluctant to pay the honest price for that quality.

Today, every bottle of olive oil in the stores is labeled "Extra Virgin" or refined oil. This is the very reason why inducement to fraud is so popular. The industry has not adopted the Virgin Olive Oil grade as a consumer product. Whoever figures this out will make a mint.

So why can't we stop the fraud and abuse olive oil suffers here in the US? A very long question with an answer that is sadly brief. No one is protecting us. You have a right to be discouraged. This industry is a big disappointment. We, as intelligent consumers, expect more but the education will come from learning firsthand about good olive oil and then teaching your friends and family. Then they, too, can stop making wasteful, costly, and unhealthy decisions about what they are putting on their food.

You cannot rely on the USDA to do anything about this at the time of this writing. It is a business-to-business (B2B) trade issue. And every year, we see settlements in the courts, often in California, where a consumer or class-action group believe they were misled into purchasing olive oil that made claims of a specific grade of quality, such as the highest grade, Extra Virgin.

But with chemical and sensory testing, those oils in question were not as advertised in the store. One of my former clients, an industrial producer of olive oil in all the grades available, voluntarily removed bottles of EVOO from shelves of retailers all over the world, including their own bottles. Those samples were air shipped to an IOC-accredited lab and tasting panel in Europe for a double-blind evaluation. Almost every sample was defective in some way. This data was shared with retail buyers, though with the names of the brands hidden. No action was taken to address this at the retail level. So the sales continued and no brands were held accountable. In the end, in America, it comes down to "caveat emptor"—let the buyer beware.

What about health claims? Extra virgin olive oil is consumed, as I have written, for two primary reasons: taste and health benefits. According to one of the most respected nutrition researchers in the US, Mary Flynn, a research dietitian and associate professor of Medicine and Clinical Research at Miriam Hospital and Brown University, who has studied the effects of extra virgin olive oil consumption on humans for decades, concludes that two tablespoons a day (at 15 ml each) of high-quality EVOO is needed to see lasting positive results[1]. But what a researcher publishes and what a producer can legally say on their package of olive oil or on their website are vastly different. Why? Because not all olive oils are created equally, so you cannot compare expected results when the comparison is between an apple and an orange. And the FDA (the regulatory arm of the US government) has very strict and narrow allowances for making claims about almost every-

---

1   Mary Flynn, PhD in published and public remarks she has made on the subject.

thing we believe is healthy for us, olive oil in particular. Yet today, walk into most any food retailer, including the "healthy claims," and you will find olive oil bottles that make flagrant claims, such as "high in polyphenols," "healthiest olive oil," or "reduces inflammation."

Simply administer your olive oil as Mary Flynn suggests: at least two tablespoons a day, consumed or prepared at low temperatures with cooked vegetables, and see the results for yourself. See how your body feels in three months. In fact, have your blood work checked for lipids (total cholesterol and triglycerides) and lipoproteins (HDL and LDL) and fasting blood glucose before you really start using better EVOO daily and then six months later. If you have been consuming extra virgin olive oil, you should see an increase in HDL, which is the healthy way to carry cholesterol in your blood. There is currently no medicine that will independently increase HDL. Some medicines work to decrease blood triglycerides and that can increase HDL slightly. But extra virgin olive oil will increase HDL and daily use will also improve HDL function, which is amazing. Daily extra virgin olive oil will also decrease your fasting blood glucose and there is evidence that it does this by decreasing insulin resistance, which means it helps your insulin to work better by getting glucose out of the blood and into the cells. And you don't need some olive oil bottler to make that claim. You know it worked because you changed your oil to a great bottle, and you saw the changes in your blood work. Increased HDL, improved metabolized glucose, anti-inflammation, and what's most compelling are the anti-oxidant properties.

What EVOO does distinctively contain are polyphenols. While these greatly vary brand to brand and bottle to bottle—depending on at least what olive is used, the growing and harvesting of the olive, the production of the oil—this is a food that does have the propensity to deliver amazing health and healing benefits, which most foods cannot. Of the phenols found in EVOO, some are more profound than others. And it is worth some of your time to check resource materials to gather more data on what polyphenols mean to us. Anti-inflammatory benefits are the more widely-known health rewards. And there is a good amount of literature about this. EVOO brands typically deliver more polyphenols when the oil is more bitter, which is usually a result of the olives being harvested earlier. I have tried oils with claims (by the producers as it is illegal to claim more than 250 mg/kg in the US) of over 3,000 mg/kg. The oil is almost inedible. But many brands you will find that I recommend will be in the 500–700 mg/kg range of total phenols. Again, buyer beware. You have to have a good bottle of oil, use it regularly, and then see how you are feeling after some time has passed. I think of polyphenols and the overall health benefits of EVOO like I do water. I know I need eight glasses a day, so I drink it. I urge you to include good quality EVOO in your daily diet too.

Note: All EVOOs do *not* deliver equal healthy attributes, and this is not a health book. You already know olive oil is good for you. We have read it for years and the research continues today, online and in print, as well as on TV in talk shows about the benefits of including "olive oil" in our diets. I agree. There is resounding evidence that populations of people whose diet is rich in specific foods, like extra virgin olive oil, have longer lives. Two of the most documented areas are Okinawa, Japan (for their vast consumption of fish), and Crete, Greece for their extreme consumption of EVOO. The last documented quantity per capita in Greece was twenty-four liters per person per year. Americans consume less than one liter per person in the US, as stated earlier in the book.

Does consumption of extra virgin olive oil equal a longer, healthier life? I'm not sure any medical professional or scholar can reasonably make this claim for certain unless they divulge the exact oil they used to make that statement. As I have stated, all olive oil and EVOO grade olive oil are subject to many problems, both before the bottling and after shipment of the product to stores. So it's best to temper expectations and just capitulate that like fresh vegetables, quality EVOO will be a healthier fat for us to consume than any other, and it makes food taste better so we should be eating it daily.

What is important is that you know how to buy the right brand. It is my recommendation that you look at none of the health claims on olive oil bottles when making a purchasing decision. Why? Because you don't need to commit to memory what claims the FDA allows or doesn't. Just assume many are disallowed and learn what you can from this book and other simple, trusted resource materials that can give you tips on how to select the best bottle you can find and afford. The FDA is very strict about health claims allowed on all foods. As it should be. There is a very narrow alley in which a bottler of olive oil can actually, legally make claims. But many still do print health claims on their packages or marketing materials to sway an innocent and uneducated consumer to choose their product. I had to learn my lesson the hard way about proper declarations of health claims on olive oil.

At a major natural foods show some years ago, I was exhibiting my Greek brand. In our booth, we had a large display with signage that implied health claims around our EVOO. In fact, we had a very reputable doctor (DO) who worked for us as a part-time chief wellness officer, and she was in this booth. Her endorsement and communication of the healthy benefits of our oils, we believed, made a big difference in the popularity of our products to the buyers who were walking around the show. We felt comfortable making more ambitious health positioning statements in an industry-only trade show that was not open to the general public.

The show opened its doors on day one and within minutes, two FDA compliance agents paid me a visit in our shiny new booth. Dressed like any two young guys walking down the street, I was almost in disbelief until they flashed me their credentials. My sphincter clenched up, as I am a do-gooder by nature and never like to run afoul of the law. They read over our booth—almost as if they were expecting something to be illegally presented. Then they jumped on their cell phones, and I saw them looking over our company website. Within ten minutes, they advised me that both the printed materials and trade show booth art, as well as my website, were not in compliance with the FDA allowable claims. They suggested I shut down my website until I could remove the dis-allowed health claims. As for the booth, they didn't make me take it down, but they warned me not to display it again. They ended by saying I was their first visit, and they planned to stop at every olive oil booth at this show. And I heard they did. And from then on, every claim I ever considered, I ran by our FDA legal team based in Chicago for their green light.

I still see brands taking advantage of health claims with every visit to the grocery store. And when I have pointed out to retail buyers that claims are being made wrongfully on products they are selling, not once has any one of them removed those items—or even addressed it, to my knowledge. I go into this in more detail in Chapter Eight, "Grocery Games," but never ever trust a label, neck hanger, social media account, or website of any olive oil producer. Even the great ones. Just don't. I have challenged producers I know and have trusted them to do the right thing. I have undertaken legal challenges with large olive oil bottlers who take advantage of unwitting consumers—and prevailed. And I have worked closely with well-known retailers to guide them to restrict brands that try to take advantage of this retail category in which managers don't know what to ask. The playing field needs to be made level. It still isn't today.

So how can you protect your purchasing power, even against the fraud and confusion on the shelves? There is an easy acronym to remember for how olive oil can be damaged:

HALT= Heat, Air, Light, Time.

These are the criminals of quality. One warning I need to share in this chapter is a strong reminder that EVOO is volatile.

"H" in HALT—Heat.

Equally as important is *not* decanting your oil into a pretty cruet, perhaps something you picked up at a cooking store or TJMaxx. These are almost always made of either clear glass or plastic and have an open pourer, which allows air into the

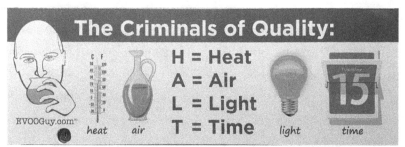

The Criminals of Quality:

H = Heat
A = Air
L = Light
T = Time

EVOOGuy.com™

heat   air   light   time

HALT at EVOOGuy® Market Stand, sign on oil cooler

bottle; this will oxidize your oil. That's the "A" in HALT. Air. By leaving a cruet on a table, especially in a clear glass container, the date when it was meant to be used by, which started in your mind the day you opened the bottle, will be long forgotten and those months become weeks, then days. The time will decay the oil, likely changing making it rancid. And light in the room (versus a dark, closed cupboard) also damages oil, so these are examples of the "L" (light) and "T" (time) that finish the HALT acronym.

Any one or a combination of these variables will lead to a defective product—one which may not be called extra virgin on the label. If the olive oil shelving section is by the hot deli case, the oils will turn bad faster. Bottles of clear glass should never be available for sale since light changes the quality quickly, and yet, you'll still find many clear containers. When I had my olive oil event business, which the COVID-19 pandemic killed, I designed the ultimate olive oil truck to drive to and use at events. The EVOOGUY Truck.

This was a Mercedes Metris, to which I had a $15,000 refrigeration unit and insulated walls added. I also insulated the ceiling and the floor of the truck for the purpose of keeping the olive oil I transported at or below 70° F. In fact, the truck had an

EVOOGuy® Truck event set-up in Florida,
over 10,000 people showed up in one night

electrical inverter, which allowed me to plug the truck up to any
electrical outlet and run the reefer unit as long as I desired. The
oils remained in a temperature-controlled environment. That's
a very good example of the lengths needed to properly care for
EVOO when outside of room temperature.

Be aware of where you are buying the oil and what you are
up against in terms of potential fraud or being duped. I tend to
group retailers (resellers) into classifications: natural/organic
stores, grocery stores, specialty/gourmet stores, mass-market
discounters, and club chains. You can add e-commerce, "olive oil
bulk" boutique stores, farmers markets, and military exchanges
as well. Some of these may have as few as two different bottles to choose from. The larger sections may have hundreds.
Your town may have a few of these places to shop or many. I do

include a reference section at the back of this book with lists of where to buy better oils. There is no simple answer to which of these many options will have a selection that is higher in quality. This reinforces the need for you to really know how to select a bottle that has the highest chance of delivering the quality you seek and are paying for. If you cannot find a brand you are satisfied with, you can do some research on the internet where there are many excellent e-trailers who specialize in selling superior oils. At the end of this book, I will provide you with my Top Brands list of the EVOO that will change your outlook forever.

EVOO FAST FACTS:

One sure way to minimize your chances of being duped is to look for seals of origin by structured consortiums, such as IGP (protected geographic indication, or a.k.a., PGI), DOP (protected designation of origin, a.k.a., PDO), and others. These organizations, typically regional to an olive growing area, protect their name and reputation by providing a seal and registration number on authorized and participating bottles for identification. While there can be some abuse, it will reduce the chances of a consumer purchasing an EVOO that isn't as presented on the label.

CHAPTER SEVEN
Defects

You can smell defects before you even become a taster. If your olive oil does not smell like freshly cut grass or tomato leaves, or sometimes banana and green almond, then you are looking at an oil with a likely defect, and it should not be used. Rancid is the primary defect and the only defect that can occur in the bottle after bottling and when the oil has undergone extensive oxidation and or exposure to heat, air, light, or time—what I referred to in the prior chapter as HALT (a common issue in the handling of oil). If you don't know what a rancid oil or food smells like, it's akin to old flour or old peanuts. You can make rancid oil at home. Take any bottle of oil you have and leave it in a window of your house in the sun for three to four days. Then smell it. You should have produced an excellent example of what rancidity smells like.

As I wrote about in the previous chapter, defects are a legal disqualification for the grade Extra Virgin. But of course, there are no penalties at this writing for violating the voluntary USDA standards. Also, even an expensive brand, where the producer takes all the right actions to ensure they bottled the best oil they could, may have gone rancid during the extensive route to market, which can take three to six months. If a bottle on the shelf does have a defect (or multiple defects), discovered by a qualified tasting panel and a chemical analysis, the product should be removed. Rancid oil is bad for you, number one, and defective oil tastes and smells bad. So *ipso facto,* chances are if you don't like the smell, that oil you just bought is *no bueno* for you.

The options from here, depending on the results of the analyses, could be that the bottles affected are downgraded to virgin, still edible and unrefined, and perfectly suitable for some cooking methods. In the worst cases, the oil could be so bad that it would be graded as *lampante.* That oil is unfit for both sale to consumers and consumption by any means, unless it is refined. But the oils may not be sold as grade Extra Virgin. You know by now that these shenanigans are misleading, unethical, and in many countries, completely illegal. In the US, olive oil standards are still voluntary, meaning the producers should label correctly, but the FDA and USDA won't hunt you down and punish you. But plenty of retailers have been sued by consumers who feel betrayed and taken advantage of. Most of these cases end up being settled. Please, think of your options as you smell your oil.

All defects are listed in the USDA's United States Standards for Grades of Olive Oil and Olive-Pomace Oil, effective October 25, 2010, and somewhat parallel the more rigid international standards of the IOC (International Olive Council). Links to these can be found on my website. These include the aforementioned rancidity, but other defects can appear, some to a greater and others to a lesser degree:

Musty/Earthy: common with those olives that fall to the ground due to ripening prior to harvest and are collected off the soil, usually with a vacuum truck, and then sent to the mill. This defect imparts a dirty aroma and taste that stays with the olives (even if they are washed prior to crushing). And there are many more examples of where the olives are defective between the tree limbs and the crushing machinery.

Muddy Sediment: common with oil left in the storage tank where sediment was conveying a very unpleasant aroma. It can also originate from dirty storage tanks that have not been properly cleaned before filling. It's the worst smell of all the defects. You will know it when you come across it.

Winey: common with olives sitting around too long before the crush becomes fermented. The oil smells like red wine.

Metallic: common with oil that had prolonged contact with non-stainless steel machinery and surfaces, leaving a faint metallic taste.

Frozen: common with oil produced using frozen olives from a freeze during harvest. It's rare but it does happen. The oil will smell a bit like snow.

Grubby: common with olives that were damaged by the olive fly prior to harvesting. Yes, often the flies are in the oil as a result of the crush. They leave an odd taste.

Fusty-Anaerobic Fermentation: one of the most common defects, caused when olives are placed in sacks where air cannot surround the olives, and they start to decay prior to production. Not a smell you will soon forget.

If your oil smells like wax, crayons, play-dough, nail polish, yeast, solvent, paint, mold, dirt, vomit, baby diapers, manure, old sweaty gym clothes, sweaty socks, black-brined olives, hay, wood, frost, stewed fruit, or even caramel, then one of these defects are in play, and this is just a short list of some of the horrible aromas that defective oils can translate.

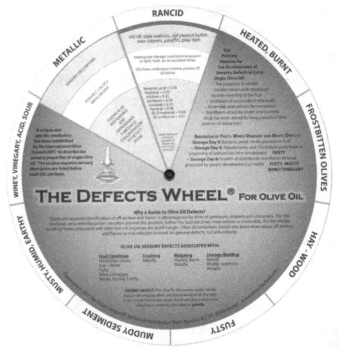

Defect Wheel (Note: Used with permission by Sue Langstaff)

Defects change the quality of the olive oil and make it less tasty, sometimes even inedible. They can also change the healthy properties the oil could have delivered. But if you do not know what to look for with a bottle of oil, or even on a spoon in a restaurant, you will keep ingesting bad oil.

These negative attributes you experience either in your smelling or tasting of the small sample will be easy to detect. The oil won't smell like the fruitiness I suggested you seek, such as green or ripe banana or fresh-cut grass—vegetal aromas. If an oil has defects, a responsible producer will sell that lot as virgin grade or sell to a refinery, which will process out the defects and prepare a more suitable oil for sale as refined olive oil (Pure, Light). Unfortunately, we can't depend on many producers to do the right thing and resist the temptation to pack the bad oil as grade Extra Virgin. They will just ignore that they have put unlawfully labeled oil in a bottle and ship it off to the United States to sell to an unwitting consumer, like yourself. So we need to reject the oil as consumers. We have the pocketbooks and the power.

Defects are measured organoleptically by trained tasters who have met the standards of qualification to sit on an accredited tasting panel, led by an even more qualified and experienced panel leader, in blind analyses of olive oils to assign grades to the oil. Tasters (as which I am trained) have developed the sensory attributes to accurately determine the positive attributes of extra virgin olive oil and assign an intensity to these on a scale from zero to ten. But they are also trained to detect negative defects, again on a scale from zero to ten.

For olive oil to make the highest level claim of grade Extra Virgin, it may *not* contain any defects. None. A median value of zero. And this expectation holds true even as bottles sit on grocery shelves up to the printed "best before dates" on the packages (unopened). This is why defects are such an important topic for me to write about and for you as a consumer to be able to find on your own, to the degree that you can, without the official training. Remember, participants of the USDA Quality Seal get away with defects of an intensity of up to two out of ten and can still make the extra virgin claim. The playing field is not fair for the consumer. But trust me, you can learn enough to get by.

Once, in an international olive oil competition I was judging, I smelled an overwhelming odor of oregano in a sample I was evaluating with my fellow judges. Now, many EVOOs are derived from olive trees where hints of herbs like mint, fruits like tomatoes and lemons, vegetables like artichokes, and nuts like almonds, as well as green grass are present. But I have never tasted an oil with such a strong predominance of oregano. You can make infused olive oil with herbs like oregano. But they cannot be legally sold as extra virgin since there was an adulteration to the oil, rendering it defective. So this was not grade Extra Virgin. The oregano aroma was so strong no other attributes could be determined. I believed that the oil this producer made probably had a problem, and to cover that up, they added some essence of oregano. That sample was disqualified by our table. This relates to a form of a defect that isn't a "classical" defect, but it is wrong to label a bottle as grade Extra Virgin with infused or flavored olive oils. Even if the well-intentioned producer used extra virgin grade olive oil as the base oil, then added the herbal or fruit infusions, these oils are now "defective" in the eyes of what the grade Extra Virgin means.

In all transparency, I have been guilty of this too. My former brand owners both insisted we call our infused options grade Extra Virgin—"Basil Extra Virgin Olive Oil" or "Chili Extra Virgin Olive Oil." All of my attempts to sway them failed. And there are producers who I adore who still sell infused olive oil as extra virgin grade. But it doesn't make it right. And if they tried to pull this off in the EU where the IOC oversees the grades with the proper oversight, unlike our USDA, those products would be disallowed for sale.

If you do discover any one or a combination of the defects listed above from smelling the oil you are about to use or have purchased, it is my recommendation that you return the bottle to the store from where you purchased it, as directed in Chapter Six.

I have a trick for most of my Olive Oil 101 classes, which may be helpful for you at the start. It emphasizes the basics of sensory science and exactly how important our sense of smell is to establishing a particular aroma. Get a red jelly bean. Cherry is best. Pinch your nose closed with one hand, and with the other, place the jelly bean in your mouth. Can you tell what flavor it is (assuming you didn't know)? You can taste the sweetness, but you cannot establish the flavor. Then release your nostrils and the familiar cherry smell radiates throughout your mouth. But is it in your mouth? Or did your nose pick up the smell when you allowed it to? Our noses contain thousands of sensory receptors, but our palates have many less. This is, in part, why, when you have a cold, you cannot smell the chicken soup everyone suggests you eat to get well. Your nasal passages are stuffed up.

When I took my first training class in Italy at the ONAOO school, Level 1, Technical Course for the Aspiring Olive Oil

Taster, in 2012, I realized how much I didn't know despite all I thought I knew! On the return trip from that week-long course in Imperia, Italy (the top of the boot as they call it), I stopped in New York City to join my partner/investor at Lucini Italia under the founding ownership, Molinos Rio La Plata, a giant food conglomerate based in Buenos Aires, Argentina, who owned an Italian pasta brand, Delverde. Delverde was hosting a kick-off event, launching a bus tour in the eastern US to promote and educate consumers about their brand and their partnership with my brand of EVOO. I was part of the executive team as host and asked to do an olive oil tasting for guests, media, and dignitaries in attendance, so we located to a back portion of the showroom. I was flattered but terrified. I was just anointed as a new "taster" by the school in Italy. Hardly prepared to share this knowledge with our valued guests yet. It was a festive evening, widely attended by many key media editors, the Italian consulate, some buyers, and our surprise keynote speaker, Gail Simmons, host of Bravo TV's most-watched show, *Top Chef*.

After the kick-off, pre-event meeting, I manned my tasting station, apportioned with the Lucini EVOO, as well as a grocery store brand that I had my staff purchase in the city, and was ready to go. My aim was to quickly impart some simple facts about what EVOO is, how it can be affected by the influences of heat, air, light, and time (HALT), and inform of the wide separation in quality and therefore, performance, between an excellent bottle of EVOO for $19 and a typical supermarket brand, at the same size, for $7. As you have learned in this book, they are both called the same thing, but the delivery of taste, positive attributes, and overall quality are light-years apart. I figured I had five minutes to make my point before I bored everyone to death.

Each touchpoint I had that evening was meaningful. The crowd around me grew from a small gathering to a crowded area. Even after I gave my spiel and we smelled and tasted (which I teach you how to do later in the book) the excellent oil compared to the traditional grocery store brand, I described both the positive attributes (fruity, bitter, and pungent) and obvious defects (fusty-anaerobic fermentation and rancid—oxidized). I could see the lights going off in these guests' heads. At the time, it helped my brand, but it also allowed me to educate, in an unofficial capacity, the curious public. It's highly likely that they, like you, have been purchasing and consuming poor quality olive oil, oil that is mislabeled as grade Extra Virgin intentionally or labeled correctly but had since turned rancid and is now unacceptable nor pleasant to consume.

So what do you do if you have a bunch of oils in the pantry that you have now determined through smell are defective? Defective oils do not need to be considered waste. If you are cooking with high heat, grade Extra Virgin is a better option, but you can make use of these defective oils, or refined oil, which comes at a much lower price (especially since you already bought it!). If a taste panel discovers an oil is not Extra Virgin, but the defects don't totally eliminate the oil from a usable status, there is the virgin grade. Perfectly acceptable. In the meantime, defects are here to stay. By the end of this book, you will be aware enough to detect some of them on your own. And your chances of continuing to support products that don't quite make the grade decrease. So why, you ask, are olive oils on the store shelves possibly mislabeled as Extra Virgin and allowed to be sold? Let the "grocery games" begin.

EVOO FAST FACTS:

Don't be tempted to purchase more EVOO than what you will reasonably need in a few months, unless the store or online retailer has an amazing deal on *quality* EVOO. It makes more sense to keep a few different intensities of fruitiness around to meet various uses. If you find with time that you lean to one particular intensity, then you may just want to stick with that.

CHAPTER EIGHT
Grocery Games

N ow that you know what you are up against with the production and distribution of oil, as well as the lack of oversight by the industry standards and government regulation, let's head into our friendly grocery stores to learn their behind-the-scenes modus operandi when selling olive oil. While ultimately, our noses (and our taste buds) can be our guide with oil, I can't stress enough the value of consumer knowledge when it comes to purchasing power. Grocery stores should be working for you and protecting you as the buyer, but they are not, so with olive oil, you need to fight back by knowing their games.

One of the questions I am asked the most when I give my Olive Oil 101 lectures is, "How do grocery chain buyers make assortment decisions for the public to choose from and how do bottles of EVOO get priced?"

The explanations are complicated but worth outlining so you can know what the buyers do and don't understand about this often maligned category in food stores. More importantly, I want to leave you with the facts and tools so *you* can supplement shortsighted decisions on the part of retail chains. The grocery games may be unstoppable, in large part, but you can see through them and make smart consumer choices for your olive oil purchases.

The primary role of every olive oil brand is to get product onto shelves at food retailers. If their brand is higher-end, like my brand Lucini Italia was, their sights are set on chains, such as Whole Foods Markets, The Fresh Market, Central Market in Texas, and even Sprouts. Some very good, disciplined, larger format grocery chains stock and merchandise better types of EVOOs too. I list many of these in the reference section at the back of this book. Volume brands that you may be familiar with are typically never found in better stores, such as retailers who focus their assortment on more unique products that deliver a better quality or experience than, say, a typical grocery store whose business model is to sell to the broader population— those who may be less choosy. These higher brands' focus is more on natural or specialty foods because the buyers realize they must offer a more curated assortment to shoppers who are willing to spend more for a product they have taken the time to research and seek out.

Let me tell you a story about my first year as president of Lucini Italia. This story shows the lengths I went to in order to stay ethical and maintain a high value with the oil I brought to the grocery stores. I can assure you, there are very few companies with internal advocates that would go to these efforts to ensure you have wonderful oil. A large discount retailer made a request for us to sell them our oil. At the time, our popular Tuscan EVOO was $17.99 for a 17 oz bottle on the market, and while we were flattered that their informal company product evaluation panel had selected Lucini Italia Premium Select as their #1 ranked extra virgin olive oil of all products they were considering to expand their assortment, we could not have the same label we sold in higher-end stores sell for a significantly lower price in these buildings. This would totally destroy our relationship with the retail partners we had patiently built into loyal supporters over many years. But this retail chain was persistent. We needed to figure out what to do to ensure we could make them happy and not ruin the rest of the market. The size of their business and the subsequent potential of incremental business growth for us were very tempting.

We planned and conducted extensive consumer research to validate that consumers indeed hoped to find a great bottle, like Lucini, on a big-box discounter's shelves, but at those discount prices. Made sense. People want good oil cheap, but as I have made clear, price indicates quality when it comes to EVOO. To get to the lower price, we just lowered our cost and justified it by selling directly to this large discount chain versus through a food distributor, which typically adds 20-plus percent gross margin of the cost to every product. And with no trade costs levied by this chain, we could also direct those savings into lowering our price.

But anyone who knew good EVOO could taste both the Lucini EVOO bottles side-by-side and realize it was the same product. So the goal was to have the same brand in the high-end and low-end stores, but the big box oil bottle would have to be of lower quality to make financial sense long-term. We had to develop a better solution.

It became evident to me after a few years (yes, years!) of searching for this lower-priced oil for Lucini—and numerous meetings with potential suppliers, many of whom were fairly sketchy characters—that we may have to make this new lower-priced EVOO from a different country. But that would defy our brand positioning. *Lucini Italia.* From day one, a brand of EVOO that had originated only from Italy. My supply office in Tuscany didn't have many suitable options. But I had one trick up my sleeve—to ask a friend, mentor, and author of the *New York Times* best-selling book, *Extra Virginity*, Tom Mueller for help. I fell to my proverbial knees and begged him for some producer names that he would trust, given his years of research into writing his book, who could help produce an oil that was good enough to be packed as Lucini Italia. But not too good! My quality consultant, Alice, joined me in Italy to meet with a very large bottler (not an olive oil producer) in the South—Bari, in the Puglia province of Italy.

Once we arrived, we met our supply agent who had driven down from Livorno to meet us. The three of us met the owners of this facility in the main offices. A typical, Italian, drab commercial office. Old furniture. A few award plaques for winning some olive oil competitions. And a very stoic look on the faces of the people. The founder and namesake of the business was a much older man, perhaps in his seventies. A younger man, in his forties, who spoke English, was their export manager.

That very odd icebreaker trip to Bari convinced Alice and me that this producer had the scale and source for decent, 100 percent Italian EVOO and could easily handle the incremental business this discounter chain had provided us while providing Lucini the pricing we needed to make the numbers work. This oil was not nearly as special as the Premium Select Tuscan EVOO we were well known for. It came from a big region known well for quantity, not as much for quality or uniqueness. It had flavor, but not nearly as fruity as our existing oil—for the lower cost we couldn't expect it to be. But there was a hitch. They could not run their filling line with our complicated, eight-sided, cus-tom-faceted Lucini bottle. Therein lay the decision: keep look-ing for a producer who can meet all our needs or compromise. We were losing money selling our great Tuscan-grown and pro-duced oil to this discount chain. So I made the tough decision to sign a supply agreement with these Pugliesi suppliers and use a standard olive oil bottle called a marasca bottle—that also denotes value—versus our fancy bottle, which cost three times more per bottle. When selling to a discount chain, every penny that can be saved and passed on to the shopper counts. Within a few months, the revised Lucini Italia Estate Select began pro-duction with our new southern supplier and was shipped to our US warehouses.

The cost savings I had discovered by finding this new bot-tler in the South meant Lucini could finally enjoy a small profit margin after years of losses. But no brand can make changes to a listed item without a face-to-face meeting with the buyers in their corporate offices. Outside of an annual business review, any meeting almost always means some type of stress. Typically, I would see a new buyer every few years. These buyers rotate from one purchasing area of the company to another every year or so. So forget about a buyer developing experience in a complicated category such as olive oil. They probably came from "soups and crackers" and after "oils" will go to "pet food." This is another type of grocery game—the juggling of buyers. The constant change is primarily so a comfort level isn't established between us and the buyer. Every buyer change requires me to start over. The meeting always starts with a review of our sales and metrics. These are available to me as a vendor through their vendor portal so I am prepared. And I was prepared for the bad news.

"Your product is selling at .25 units per week per store, compared to national brand movement of 20 units per week on average," said the buyer. Then the blank stare. Vendor intimidation to gain leverage in the meeting must be part of their training. Well, that didn't work on me. I had my standard answers ready for them.

"Your buying team chose us a few years ago to be in your stores. They knew we were more expensive than the other offerings, but they selected us for our quality and authenticity. Not because we were going to be a sales leader." The buyer knew and expected my pat reply. But they had to ask and I had to answer. Grocery games.

The meeting continued as expected. The buyer pushed back on the new oil, even though when we tasted it with her, she really didn't understand the difference. I did. She didn't love the new marasca bottle. It was a plain bottle, the most popular used for olive oil. But it was inexpensive and worked on our new producer's line. She felt this was a departure from the original buying decision. Be that as it may, this was not a visit about negotiating but about making a declaration. Survival was at stake for my small brand, not for them. As many meetings go, it lasted less than thirty minutes. It took an entire day to get to their office for a half-hour meeting. After I reviewed our necessary changes and the competition that existed on her shelves, we were still heads above all the other olive oils with regard to quality. And the bottle remained there for another seven years until we sold the brand. This discounter's consumers had a long run of availability of a great 100 percent Italian EVOO at impossibly low prices, but the journey to get the product to them is very complicated and expensive.

The next olive oil review at the same discounter landed me in another uncomfortable situation with another new buyer. I had been to their stores weeks prior to my annual meeting. In every store I checked in the Miami area, where my office was, stacks of a national brand of olive oil in a giant two-liter bottle were being sold next to Lucini bottles. I was shocked. This isn't something this retailer often did with olive oil. The bottle was made of PET (plastic), which is the first sign of cheap oil. The plastic bottle was tinted a deep, dark green to deceive the consumer into believing that the oil was green, another sign of misdirection. The label showed the famous image of a Tuscan hillside and a church. However, when you turn the bottle around, the declaration of origin states, "Product of Spain." Another warning sign: a Spanish oil (and its Spanish brand) utilizing an

Italian landscape as their front label. The lettering on the front label was dark black, printed on that deep green background—impossible to read.

Then I looked at the price. Eight dollars for the two-liter bottle. That equates to $4 a liter, or $2 for a half-liter (17 oz/500 ml), the size most consumers choose. Two dollars, versus my Lucini Italia EVOO, actually from Italy, on the shelves for $9.99. A bargain. But still five times the price as this oil on the large display. But then I looked really hard—the words popped into my brain like a starburst. "Premium Extra Virgin Olive Oil" was printed in gold letters, easy to read, and "Sunflower Oil" printed below that in black letters, impossible to read. *What? Seriously?* I had never seen, and haven't seen since, such apparent fraud. *How can they get away with this?* And how could this huge retailer allow this? I took a lot of pictures with my phone and sent them to my excellent FDA law firm to review it for compliance with existing labeling laws.

At the next annual review, again with a new buyer, I asked about the olive oil promotion in the stores I had witnessed. I had enlarged photos of the display and a close-up image of the bottle. He confirmed that he had booked that deal, and it meant a significant savings to his shopper. For which, I assumed, he meant a bonus for him at some point. Buyers are always incentivized to lower costs and increase sales and gross margins (profit). He actually looked proud of the photo. Well, his day was about to change for the worse.

In sharing the legal opinion from my lawyer that the company was promoting an illegally labeled product, my goal was not to humiliate the buyer. My actual potential gain from this was nominal. But when confronted with information that our sales are not adequate, it's appropriate for me to have a reasonable counter. I laid out my case. I shared copies of all the documentation, and I actually had a live bottle of that oil with me. Indeed it broke my heart to purchase one for this meeting at their large corporate store a few blocks from their head office, but I was taught early on by the Lucini founders—if you have to buy a sample of a competitor's oil, always purchase one of yours as well, which I did. I offered to do a taste comparison, the mislabeled oil and Lucini Estate Select EVOO, 100 percent Italian. They declined, saying they don't "taste in the morning." I stated my case about consumer confusion, one really easy explanation why my sales would be low, and asked the buyer what he could do about it. (They were not the only retailer selling this product—almost every grocery chain I checked had some size of this same bottle on their shelves). He looked me square in the face, and with the typical buyer expressionless look said, "We are an aircraft carrier, and it takes us a long time to make a turn in another direction."

That was it. No explanation. No apology. No concurrence that what they were doing seemed both unethical and possibly illegal. It hurt every real bottle of properly labeled EVOO on their shelves, not just ours. Ultimately, that promotion ended, but the bottles remained on the retailer's shelves. My last remedy was to send a letter of dispute, drafted by my FDA attorney, to the brand owners of that apparently fraudulent and possibly illegally labeled product. A company fifty times bigger than mine. I hoped that their sense of right and wrong would prevail, and perhaps we could expect a level playing field one day. Well, that day came five years later when they made the simple, yet somewhat legal change to their label—taking off the black lettering that said, "Sunflower Oil" and making it gold like the Extra Virgin lettering. In reality, that oil was probably 99 percent sunflower oil and 1 percent virgin olive oil. Remember, it cannot be labeled extra virgin grade if there are any changes to the oil, such as blending it with something other than another extra virgin grade oil. These are grocery games with high stakes. But I had become quite the player of the games that I faced.

I tell you this story because it covers many of the nuances and potholes of the olive oil business. Frankly, I could never list here all the grocery games that are played. At least fifty come to the top of my mind, but covering a few that I have personally experienced and others I know are evident after a career in the food industry will continue to assist you in being a smart shopper. A hidden mechanism exists underneath your oil getting to the shelf.

Take for instance, "FIFO: First In First Out." At the point of sale, where the product rests on a shelf, waiting for its new home, grocery stockers can further compromise olive oil quality by not rotating the stock. This means, simply, when a new case of oil comes in, they should check the "best before date" (if it has one—remember they are not legally required for olive oil, so buyer beware), and if it is longer than the goods on the shelf, they should place the newly delivered items in the back of the slot and pull the older ones to the front. But many times, this isn't done. So the older products are hidden and blocked by the newer delivery, and thus, the oil sits on the shelf longer. If you see bottles at the very back of a shelf when inventory is low, don't take them. They may have been there for a long time. The only inventory that gets consistently rotated on shelves is with "jobbers" who do a good job for cookies, snacks, and soda. They can take in cases of fresh stock and take products back that are expired or close to expiry and then sell them at a factory store. And unlike wine, olive oil does not get better with age. So always look at the "best before dates" of the bottles in the front and the back. I suggest picking the one with the longer "best before date," irrespective of where they are on the shelf.

There is another grocery game I call "Musical Chairs." I related a bit of this earlier in this chapter. Grocery (also known as center store) attracts buyers who are *not* product experts like their colleagues in the full-service departments. Often, they are younger, have a leaning toward accounting, and are just passing through to get to another desk inside the purchasing department. One of the larger mass retailer chains in America rotated buyers every six months. Often, they were just out of college. They were cheap labor, ambitious, dressed well, and smart people . . . but just getting started. Every visit to their head office to call on them was very frustrating. They didn't care to learn about my products; they didn't understand why our pricing was higher than national brands (which were often much lower quality), and once I started to make some progress with one of them, they were suddenly gone, and I was moved to another buyer, who said they needed time to learn the category before they could make any additions or changes.

These are the buyers at larger food chains that have the authority to make assortment decisions. They are not trained properly to understand the products being presented, from the ingredients themselves to the manufacturing processes, nor to the valuation of the finished product. But in my thirty-plus years of representing foods to buyers, less than 5 percent actually understood the foods they purchased for their stores. And in olive oil, I would decrease that to 2 or 3 percent. Almost none of the buyers to whom I have presented understand, care about, or can properly investigate a product or brand to determine how it will complement their section. And in grocery stores, besides the full-service departments (e.g., the deli, meat, seafood, and even flowers), food isn't managed by product experts. The full-service, perishable departments are managed by experts who have years, if not decades, of specialized training and experience buying for their category. At retail grocery stores, the category managers (buyers) do nothing to prevent items from making it to their shelves. There is no discernment or opinion. If brands are willing to pay the price of admission, will keep their prices low, promote their products frequently, and meet demand, they can get space on the grocery store shelves. Low quality? No problem. Trade buyers of olive oil could have gone from selling greeting cards to tampons, and in six months, they are onto cookies and crackers and beer. If you are an olive oil manager, you buy the center store—relish, condiments. A highly technical food with the benefits of taste and health, but if it has a defective taste and aroma and may not qualify to be labeled as EVOO grade with no benefits, why are they buying it? Moreover, why are *you* buying it?

Another game is we call the "Strike Zone." Take a look, next time you are in a typical grocery or discount chain store, in the olive oil section for the higher-priced bottles. They are almost never easy to find. Often, they have been merchandised on the bottom or very top shelves. This is by design. The retailer wants you, the shopper, to purchase from them where the product is easiest to locate—the middle shelves. This is referred to as the "Strike Zone." Typically the brand leaders, the store's private label products, and best sellers reside in this section. But if you are seeking the best products that stores sell, irrespective of price, then look harder. They may be on the shelves, but not convenient to find. Thus, low prices, which usually lead to best sales, also earn a brand the best shelf placement. So the more artisanal, perhaps even most authentic products will always be seen as an assortment enhancer to the chain. And this is exactly why the large discount chain wanted Lucini so intently. Not to grow their sales but to build a more well-rounded, curated olive oil section.

There has been an uprising of specialty olive oil boutiques that sell proprietary olive oil to unwitting consumers. I call this grocery game "Dress for Success." A well-intentioned entrepreneur is romanced into "a second career" with some of their retirement money and uses it to open a bulk olive oil shop. They then dupe the consumer into buying fancified oil that is often not even close to extra virgin. I'm sure you have either seen or been in one of these oil boutiques. They sell soap, bath salts, and olive oil. That oil in the highly-designed bottle is purchased as bulk olive oil in drums from a wholesaler. They transfer some liters of this oil into stainless steel *fusties* containers (like the Old-World samovars, used to serve coffee). There is rarely nitrogen or argon gas used in these fusties to protect the oil from oxidation (aging)—and no telling how long that oil has sat in this dispenser or when the dispenser was last cleaned. They then charge a consumer more for a bottle than you would expect to pay. Prices do range, but in their case, it's a seller's market. How would you, as a layperson, know what that oil is worth? Moreover, how can you judge if the oil is even any good? They may assist you with a tasting, depending on the store. Do you know how to taste? Do they? And now that we see olive oil bulk stores popping up in towns all over the US, do we also need mustard shops? Catsup stores? Where does it end? Sadly, many of these entrepreneurs go out of business in their first year. The reality is, really great EVOO can be found in your town at the grocery store. You just need some skills to help you find it and then evaluate the purchase. Knowledge of the games, labeling, and how to taste will provide all you need to have purchasing power. And you will never feel like a sucker again.

Some years ago, I built an interesting EVOO business for Gaea North America with an uber-large club chain in the West. I had a buyer who just "got it." He found me exhibiting Gaea at a trade show, and from day one, we clicked. He quickly approved my product for a test in his regional stores. Getting into that chain and understanding their universe of selling to them is far more complex. Inclusion required an experienced food broker who knew the buyers and could navigate the paperwork. I met with almost every regional buyer all over the country and the national olive oil buyer in their club chain headquarters. Yet, only a few ended up purchasing from me. Their larger focus was on private labels, with only a smattering of what they call "rotational" products. The business I was building, while unstable in consistency, added a lot of value to my company through credibility, revenue, and visibility—all very valuable. This buyer had no hidden costs for a brand. No slotting fees for a pallet of your goods to sit on their floor for purchase. There were some demo costs, that's about it. And by charter, this chain could not add more than a 14 percent up-charge (markup) to a product. That is extremely attractive to a consumer. That's why over 100 million people pay an annual fee to get into their doors.

In 2018, my last year at Gaea North America as CEO before they closed the business, I had convinced the national buyer of this club chain to visit our olive groves in Greece—our "secret sauce," what made our olive oil special and worthy of a larger discussion. My goal was for the big-box chain to consider Gaea as a provider of Greek private-label EVOO, rather than the supplier they had. Their existing supplier did not produce oil in Greece; they had it made for them. And this chain always prefers direct manufacturing versus what we refer to as "co-pack," where someone else makes it for the brand who then resells it to the chain.

I was honored this buyer would visit. In fact, the buyer brought along their direct boss. So I invited our US broker for this giant chain to come and participate in the meeting. I flew from Miami to Crete via London and Athens. The meeting was originally set for half a day, starting in the early morning. We would take a tour of our groves at harvest, pick some olives for the photo opportunity, visit the crushing and bottling facility where we make our oil, then head to the office for lunch and a business discussion. It was timed to the minute because they had to come to Crete for the visit and had to fly right out.

After no less than five changes to their itinerary prior to the trip, our half-day of education and knowledge building was reduced to two hours. We were notified the day before their visit of this reduction. So we quickly adjusted. When they arrived, we took them to a nearby plot of land with olive trees and showed them how the Old-World method of handpicking and using hand-assisted processes for olives still works. And they both had a hand in picking some fruit as well.

Then to the bottling plant for a quick tour, and we used the business office of the plant to enjoy a traditional Greek lunch and have a business meeting. The whole process was abbreviated, but I believe we demonstrated our skills and abilities, and we offered very low prices to entice them to give us their business for 2019. The meeting ended at the time they requested we conclude by. They hurried out, leaving behind the branded Gaea ball caps and much of the business materials we had prepared for them to take.

A few weeks went by, and neither my broker nor I had heard anything from them. Which seemed odd, given the ramp-up (for months) to this presentation in Crete and the effort and expense our Greek team went to. Finally, I was told that the buyer is no longer on the olive oil desk and that no announcement had been made as to who was taking over. But clearly, all the trouble we had all gone to, to entice and educate them on a product they desired to change suppliers with, was for naught. I never heard a word from them. Not even a thank you. And in later months, when the new national olive oil buyer was appointed, we were told he wasn't making any changes and was satisfied with their current supplier.

This grocery game I call "Hide and Seek." Except it's the other way around. They sought us out, and then they hid. All of the efforts a brand uses to build relationships with inexperienced buyers, such as at trade shows, corporate office visits, olive oil trainings (which I gave away to dozens of chains to improve their product knowledge), are all added costs that a brand must invest to educate and hope the buyer takes these learnings to improve their assortment and better understand the category . . . those costs end up in the price of the product, of course. You, the consumer, ultimately pay for them. If business was done with educated, knowledgeable buyers who understood the category and could make qualified decisions about products based on facts, millions of dollars could be saved in the pony show for the brands. Those savings could be used by the brands to pay the farmers more for the olives used to make EVOO, which is an incentive for them to grow and harvest better fruit. Or lower the price of the oil on the shelf, making the purchase consideration more attractive for the consumer.

The best place a consumer can buy their bottle of olive oil is directly from the producer. You can cut out all the middlemen and associated costs. The caveat is that it's harder to purchase from a producer if they don't have an e-commerce site. Alternatively, an e-tailer, like Amazon or other more boutique-type resellers, will give you access to more producers than on the grocery store shelves. I have my own e-commerce site where I sell my brand of EVOO.

Be warned that not all e-commerce businesses are the same. Caution must always be exercised when purchasing on the internet—even from Amazon. I have purchased a number of bad bottles from Amazon. It's a function of the time: the products sit in warehouses, and the temperature where the goods were stored and the packaging the bottles were shipped in all matter. With the arrival of social media and heavy advertising on most of the platforms we see every day, there are many shenanigans being played, which you, as an unwitting olive oil shopper, may fall prey to.

What e-commerce will save a consumer is a lot of fat (extra cost) that the producer is spending at regular retail to survive from one year to the next. And there are far fewer, if any, games. From the annual product review process to slotting fees (typically the cost of one case of oil at wholesale per store) to promotions, some as deep as BOGO (buy one, get one free), to paying to be in flyers and off the shelf on an end-cap, the list is long. When you see those big displays at Whole Foods for a two-week promotion, that can cost a brand upwards of $25,000. Who ends up paying for that? Another grocery game, "Monopoly," gives you the answer. You try to move your product around the board, and if you land in the wrong spot, BAM, another cost.

There is a future for quality/specialty EVOO. I even believe some stores do a very good job of merchandising EVOO. Like Central Markets in Texas, owned by the HEB chain. Or Eataly, which is in some larger cities in the US, a wonderfully curated assortment of only Italian olive oils. Most you can easily trust. But the only sure way as a consumer you will ever feel like you are not being bamboozled by a chain or brand is to learn how to taste and smell, as I have related before. Because any olive oil, unless you buy it from the mill, freshly made, can turn bad and the resultant oils can be as great as excellent to as poor as inedible. I am sorry to give such a bleak report on the lies and deception by most of the brands on the shelves you see every trip to your grocery store and how little product knowledge the retailers have about the very product they sell. You are not protected by grocery stores and big-box or club chains. The answer is to make you, the consumer, less of a victim. We all are entitled to get what we pay for. Just like we would never purchase or eat a grey piece of spoiled meat left in the meat case at the grocery store, nor should we be taken advantage of by purchasing some mysterious bottle of olive oil making promises it cannot keep. I am a foodie. Many of you are too. But in this day and age, we must take a little time to know something about the foods we buy and serve our family and friends. My takeaway is that olive oil certainly is a "slippery business," as Tom Mueller coined in his *New Yorker* olive oil story in the mid-2000s.

So the only way to win the game in the retail world is to be the best expert they don't want you to be. Learn to be an amateur olive oil taster. That's where we will start your education. Game on!

EVOO FAST FACTS:

You must resist the olive oil sold at grocery stores where there are huge stacks of bottles laying on top of each other in a bin, or next to each other on an end-cap shelf. Usually, all of the various grades of these oils, from the lowest refined olive oil to the extra virgin that may claim to be "Premium" or "Organic," are all the same price. The fact is—they don't cost the same to produce and aren't worth the same, so why are they all selling for the same sale price? Yes, this is another game, "The Price Isn't Right."

CHAPTER NINE

Whose Opinion Do I Trust?

Let's face it . . . people buy products that have won awards and competitions or received positive critiques from influencers and guidebooks. In fact, consumers usually don't even know if the competition or the award is credible before they buy the product. They don't take the time to Google the competition but simply assume that they wouldn't be lied to. Now that you have read about grocery games and label deception, I bet you are going to pause before you are lured by that gold sticker on the EVOO bottle you reach for. If not yet, let me regale for you some stories of my own so you can see where some "award cred" will get you.

There are literally hundreds of ways a brand can help its product to become more recognizable through a variety of competitions, influencers, and guidebooks. Most pay to be seen and judged. Invariably, once a product has received recognition, the producer typically bestows the licensed seal or award artwork on the label or on a paper neck hanger, assuming the end-user, you, will believe the product is a better choice than, perhaps, another option without the emblem. Some ratings and rankings in the food world are highly credible and recognizable, such as the Michelin Guide, which bestows stars for top chefs and restaurants. This resource is reliable and well respected by diners worldwide to recognize the quality and value of a fine dining restaurant.

If you don't know how to taste, then invariably you may believe these accolades validate the oil, but if it smells off, it is off, and you should return it to the store!

What you need to ask yourself is, "Do I know what this competition or seal on the bottle means? Is it legit? Does the oil I'm considering purchasing resemble the oil that won this award?" Olive oil awards, seals, and guides, unlike the famed Michelin Guide, are not related to a brick and mortar location, where, as a diner, you can actually experience the foods, ambiance, and gravitas that earned the chef their notoriety.

Olive oil is a single product, one which changes vastly over time and distance, and which is highly unlikely to remotely resemble the submission the brands made many months before the evaluation. Therefore, the best bet to determine if a bottle of olive oil deserves a gold star is you, as the judge and jury, with your smelling and tasting senses. Regardless of any award or recognition, if you don't love the product, then it isn't an award winner to you.

There are dozens of EVOO competitions—some I respect and some I don't. Most accept hundreds of entrants, all of which must be tested by the producer. Many are about making money rather than making sure you, as the consumer, are getting the best olive oil. It seems every month another country or region is launching another competition. Less scrupulous competitions will recruit people with little experience for the unpaid roles of judges so the real costs are minimal. The process becomes concerning with these examples of competitions where the judges are overworked, tasting more than thirty samples in a day and, therefore, cannot be objective later in the judging day when their palates and noses are tired. Competitions who give out so many awards because their scoring system allows for these practices are not really recognizing the best of the best. They just want their entrants to be satisfied so they will submit again next year.

More times than I care to count, I have seen bottles on store shelves with award or guidebook emblems that are many years old—well past the year in which the producer won that recognition, and in some cases, the producers have since made a whole different production year of oil. This is downright misleading. Stores shouldn't allow this form of marketing but regulations are not in place, especially with EVOO. The store management could simply allow one year to sell through the product in inventory but no more than that. Take a look next time you're in a specialty or natural foods superstore for bottles with award emblems that are many years past the date of the medal. Those are brands I suggest you never purchase.

There is also no oversight for these awards. The competition executives decide on a panel leader (*cappo*) and usually, the cappo will choose their judges. A judging table usually consists of five people: four judges and a table leader, who keeps the process of evaluating the samples moving and helps break up the inevitable debates that occur. Judges should not taste more than thirty samples in a six-hour day to allow for the palate to rest. But as I stated, not all competitions follow these parameters and can overwork their judges. This does lead to fatigue in the mouth and does result in inaccurate scores.

I have had the opportunity to be a judge at a major olive oil competition in 2020 and 2021. The samples to be evaluated are always prepared double-blind, meaning the people who open the bottles and document them are not the same people who dispense the samples into tasting glasses and bring them to the judges. The samples have codes on the bottles that we (the judges) use to keep track of the scores. Judges should be well-trained "professional tasters." Those who have demonstrated expertise and have had excellent training.

Many samples were excellent. And we doled out medals. Only a few of our 100 samples in 2020 made it to the platinum level, the highest score. I would have loved to get my hands on those oils for my own use, but I was not allowed to know who they were. In 2021, my table of judges found none worthy of Platinum. However, more than 30 percent failed to even meet the EVOO standard and were disqualified.

These competitions are very important to the producers. They enter their best and hope for a winner. They can then use the awards to generate interest in their products. They consider these winners a bespoke item that is worthy of more aggressive marketing. But there are also many submissions that are disqualified as *lampante* (not EVOO grade). These are always a disappointment for us as judges to have to taste.

So that's wonderful news that there are competitions that are legit with tasters like myself who have been trained! Yes and no. The issue is that even if one of the olive oils won a legitimate award from a reputable competition, that is *not* the same olive oil you, as a consumer, will ever see in a store or shipped to you from an e-commerce site. Those oils have taken a longer road to get to you and will have substantially changed in quality. What many producers can do for the actual competition is pick their very best oil of the harvest and sequester it in a separate Inox stainless steel tank, often referred to as a "competition tank." These silos are smaller than the production ones, kept inside a temperature-controlled room, and flushed with an inert gas, such as nitrogen or argon, to remove any air that can oxidize the oil—essentially reducing aging. When it comes time to send samples, bottles are hand-labeled, the oil is decanted into the bottles, which then are usually capped with nitrogen again—if available—and then boxed with chill packs to prevent heat from affecting the oil sample. They are sent expedited to the competition for the next steps. Again, this is oil you will *never* see on the store shelves. I am the first to admit, when I was a producer for Lucini and Gaea, I submitted my brands to competitions over the years and celebrated our wins, sharing the good news with store and chain buyers. I wanted these awards on the bottle.

One well-known, domestically-held olive oil competition I would attend is the NYIOOC (New York International Olive Oil Competition) World event based in New York City every spring. This event is organized by an industry stalwart who also owns the leading olive oil e-magazine and an olive oil sommelier tasting program. They have over 1,000 entrants each year from over twenty-six countries. The US being the largest importer of olive oil in the world makes this award very attractive to producers, both large and small. I can tell you now: I believe that oils bearing these seals of adornment mean nothing and should mean nothing to the consumer. The industry is celebrating itself. The best practice for good competition with the consumer in mind is to select the samples right off the store shelves. Really bring the chain of distribution into the conversation, and make the efforts of the producers more widely known to the consumers. What makes this solution impossible is that most of the brands that submit are not available in stores. Thus, as a second guard rail, I would further suggest that only oils that are sold to the public be considered for competition. This would be validated by the competition organizer prior to judging. All too often, I have seen products win awards that produce a thimble full of oil just to win a medal. How is this fair and appropriate to a producer who must produce thousands or more liters of high-quality oil for sale?

I already came into the olive oil business a skeptic of food awards because of a sketchy experience I had as an executive in the food industry. The American Taste Awards, now called Chef's In America Awards, is a national competition of food and beverages from hundreds of categories. I was approached in the early 2000s by the then founder, Chef Jessie Sartain (now deceased), when I was an executive for a major organic breakfast foods company. He met me at a trade show we attended. It was explained to me that we should enter our cereals and waffles and why. His sales packet showed that many of the brands who had won in the years past were category leaders, and they licensed the award emblem for their packages to improve consumer confidence. I was told about their highly notable judging staff and the associated costs. After the show, I received a follow-up call again from Chef Sartain's staff. I was a skeptic but decided to take a leap and submit one cereal and one waffle to see how we ended up. We were being judged against mainstream foods, not just organic, so it would be helpful for me to see, in a truly blind competition, if our taste would hold up.

Months later, I was contacted. We had won bronze (placed third place) for the waffles. The cereal didn't place. I was discouraged but understood. Heck, organic foods twenty years ago did not taste or have the "mouth feel" they do today. But the competition reminded me that if the other two winners ahead of our waffles didn't elect to purchase the license to use their seal (emblem), then I could. That bit left me perplexed, but I ignored it. Not long after that call, I was contacted again. This time, I was told indeed, neither of the two other winners—one of whom was a direct competitor and the other, a national brand leader, had won the gold—wished to license the medal. So if I chose to, for around $20,000 for a year, (you can even pay a 50 percent discount for year two and keep the award, and they will skip the annual judging of that category for you—how convenient), I would be moved to gold place. *How fishy,* I thought at the time.

For this fee, our waffles received the "Gold Medal" for best-tasting waffles in America. Our founder was pretty impressed. We could use the award art on the packaging, sales materials, and website (no social media back then). Plus, a ticket was included for me and one person to attend the award ceremony, a black-tie event, at Carnegie Hall in New York City, where I would receive the award on stage and give a one-minute acceptance speech. Then we could participate in an after-party event in the penthouse of the Hilton Hotel on Broadway, where we would be given a table to sample our product to all guests and media. I thought, how valuable—everyone wants to eat dry waffles with their champagne! But I let my cynicism rest and attended both the awards event and the after-party. The only positive memory I can relate about that entire fiasco was that next to my table in the penthouse after-party, tequila was being sampled and a very well-known founder was pouring it. They won "Best Tequila" that year. I'm not a big drinker and remembered I had a 5:30 a.m. return flight home the next morning, but I decided to have a few shots with this guy, and we both made fun of the event and the organization we had supported with our licensing fee. My new friend seemed to take a shot and a photo with almost everyone who came to his table. Around 11:00 p.m. that night, I called it quits (after three shots), closed my table, and left. The founder, who was also a singer, was still going strong. What a brave soul, making the most of an event we both felt was basically a scam in my opinion.

The next morning, I arrived very early at BWI airport and had a long drive back to Virginia, where I lived. I got into my car and turned on the radio to listen to my favorite radio personality, Howard Stern, only to hear him say their planned guest that morning was supposed to be the same founder I had spent the evening with . . . but he had been at an event the night before and drank until the wee hours of the morning so was too hungover for the interview! I had to laugh. But in the end, a lesson was learned: I did end up getting lit with this guy on his "Gold Medal" tequila, but no more awards for me.

So where does a consumer of olive oil find the most credible and objective opinions about olive oil? Magazines (print and digital), where no fees are paid, and real editors who make a living evaluating food and writing about it and that judge the oils—known as "earned media." It is preferred that they work with industry professionals who can guide their process. Three such highly credible publications are *Cooks Illustrated, America's Test Kitchen,* and *Consumer Reports.* Their test kitchens don't accept samples from manufacturers. They actually go to stores and buy products off of the shelves, as I mentioned earlier in this chapter. My brands have done well in these magazines. But I do feel that the evaluators' personal preferences may get in the way of fair and unbiased evaluations. For example, many Americans will feel bitterness in their mouth and think the oil is bad. Some bitterness can mean there is a problem. But mostly, a bitter experience is a positive attribute. Editors can judge an oil incorrectly if they do not understand bitterness and pungency (the pepperiness in the back of one's throat experienced by many world-class EVOOs). But all in all, I find their reports helpful to consumers, and in the end, that's what matters most.

There are also many excellent social media influencers who do know what EVOO is and how to best share their knowledge with the public. There seem to be new influencers cropping up every day, so be sure that whomever you watch has a strong, working knowledge about olive oil.

Most press, if they are approached by a good public relations agency or firm, will write a nice piece about a product they receive for consideration. In the last fifteen years, I have enjoyed billions of media impressions for my various brands. Indeed, I have tasted with Martha Stewart in her studios and with MSNBC, Cheddar TV, and countless magazines, newspapers, radio shows, and more.

Editors need content. But there have been times when even well-intentioned media have gotten it wrong. And this, like competitions that aren't really awarding products honestly, can mislead consumers, especially naive ones.

One such example was on *The Dr. Oz Show*. Dr. Oz, a respected doctor (cardiologist) and Greek native, had an episode of his show some years ago with a few olive oil experts. One was Dan Flynn, who, at the time, was the executive director of the UC-Davis Olive Center in California. The show had decided to present their own "quality test," without being tested or proven by anyone, that if you refrigerate a bottle of EVOO, and the oil doesn't congeal, it isn't truly EVOO grade. I learned later from Dan Flynn that he objected to this seemingly falsely presented test and that the taping of the show had to stop to allow for hours of debate with the producers. Sadly, the show did air this claim. I was at Lucini Italia at the time, and immediately after the show aired, I was called dozens of times by my staff, customers, brokers, and even consumers. They all wanted to know if this at-home test worked; many exclaimed that they tested their Lucini oil, and it didn't congeal in this "refrigerator test," and they felt cheated. Even the buyer at a reputable family grocery chain in the Northeast (and Washington D.C.) called me to come to their head offices in upstate New York to dispel this myth (or fake news, as we say now) with their head nutritionist

. . . . or fear discontinuance. I was able to put their concerns to rest. Within a few weeks of airing, the show apparently had to make an on-air retraction after pressure from trade groups and producers alike flowed in. I had thought that was the last time I would cross paths with that show, which I now considered part of the disinformation problem olive oil had.

Some years later, as I was flying from another trade show in California to Rome via New York, I received an urgent email on the plane from my PR agency in New York City, asking if I could change my plans and delay my flight to Rome for a taping with Dr. Oz about olive oil. My blood pressure went up again. I inquired what it was about, and all they said was a producer had a hole and needed an expert and asked if I could fill in. The story was about how to tell a good oil from a bad one. It took me less than five minutes to decline. No way did I want to be part of that show. Given the mess of the "refrigerator test," I expected there could be problems. And the upside didn't seem worth it to me. I continued onto Rome.

Months later, that episode aired. They had replaced me with a young woman, who I thought had minimal industry experience, and the show didn't even acknowledge the brand she worked for. The episode targeted imported brands of EVOO, which they considered the most at risk for fraud. My brand at the time, Lucini Italia, was from Italy, so now I see what their interest in me was—to defend my own quality. They used this replacement person to support their position. Well, they didn't disclose that she worked for one of the largest California olive oil producers and may have had some bias about imports. Both she and the show were quickly sued by a leading olive oil association. The case was quietly settled, with an apology from the show and no findings of wrongdoing. I had dodged a bullet.

So if we can't trust so many sources, what are reliable ways to seek top-quality olive oil? EVOO has two guides that are highly recognized and respected. Neither has much consumer awareness. These are trade publications. The publishers do try to help, but for the layperson, having an annual guidebook to help you discern what oil you may prefer is a stretch. These books carry more importance for the trade, the olive oil businesspeople—buyers, bottlers, producers, importers, and retailers. The most notable is the annual Flos Olei guide, produced annually by Marco Oreggio in Italy. It recognizes its "Top 500" producers for the year, with special awards for the Top 20, Best Farm, Best Chef, etc. They translate it into English as well. This really is the gold standard. The scoring ranks from a minimum of 80 points to a perfect score of 100. They have held an annual event every December in Rome, where the award ceremony is held, followed by two days of tastings with the Top 20 products. I have attended as many of these as I can. For me, meeting these producers is like going to see the Rolling Stones and having a back-stage pass. Many have become my friends. Giorgio Franci is there at his table every year.

EVOOLEUM is the second guide, based out of Madrid, Spain. The publishers of this guide are also the publishers of *Mercacei*, a monthly magazine about olive oil, and they hold an annual competition. This guide is less well known, even though Spain is the largest olive grower and producer of olive oil in the world. By a lot. Their panel of judges is impressive, and the oils that have been recognized as their winners are arguably fantastic selections.

Regardless of the book, a typical US consumer has no access to either of them and very little interest. And if, by chance, you did, the top-ranked extra virgin olive oils are hard to find. But if you are an olive oil nerd like me, some of them can be found. It requires some searching. And remember, the oil you find and buy won't be like the sample the judges tasted. As a consumer, your very best approach to verifying the veracity and quality of *any* extra virgin olive oil is, as I have explained, in learning the basics of choosing, smelling, tasting, and evaluating the particular bottle you purchased. Period. Do not rely on or be swayed by awards, guide books, emblems on products, and in many cases, media or paid influencers. If olive oil producers really care about their quality, they should use the money they spend on all these awards and guides and invest it in improving the quality of handling of their packaged or bulk oil between bottling/toting facilities and the retail stores or restaurants. So much of the quality is lost here.

You will now need to trust your palate. Trust your preferences. You have now become an olive oil judge for your household.

EVOO FAST FACTS:

Olive oil isn't just for us to eat. There are more brands of skincare that use olive oil, even extra virgin grade as an ingredient, than I can count. We know what's good for us inside could be just as good for us on the outside. And the skin is our largest organ. So utilizing EVOO right out of the bottle on our skin may help turn back the clock or be a simple beauty aid. Women often use olive oil to remove eye makeup with a Q-Tip. Europeans massage EVOO into their faces routinely. It's the purest moisturizer nature can provide.

CHAPTER TEN

Master At-Home Taster, At Last!

A h, finally. The moment I have been waiting for: to make you a master "at-home taster." I hope you are incensed and educated enough thus far in the book to take your purchase power back into your hands with EVOO. With the facts that I have shared—from the trees to the grocery aisles— you can no longer question the fraudulence that runs rampant in the olive oil industry, as well as why certain oil is high quality and others are just crap. Therefore, the time has finally come where you take the only power you ultimately have to protect the quality of the extra virgin olive oil you bring into your home and serve your family, which is to learn to be a master at-home consumer and taster!

You will now combine what you learned about the basics of smelling and add to your expertise tasting and evaluating EVOO at home, without having to attend a course or school. Your time is valuable and limited. This I understand, but with as much olive oil as Americans are bringing home weekly, this simple process will bring the power of consumer knowledge into your culinary journey. Without taking up too much of your time, we can help you ensure your purchasing decisions are made as intended.

When you open your newly purchased bottle of EVOO, you experience either the wonderful aromatic realities of what you purchased or the defects, which are now fairly easy to detect since we attuned your smell to what good olive oil is and what has possibly become defective. You may still not be sure you can trust your nose so after we do our smell test, I have the added step of tasting. So save that receipt, and now, let's give that cap a twist.

As you know, opening the bottle will begin the degradation clock since you have now introduced air into the bottle and released any nitrogen or argon that a good producer may have used to slow down the aging process, so we need to do the tasting immediately. We will smell the samples first, as our nose is far more accurate than our mouths are. Americans are not fond of putting oil directly in their mouths. I can partly understand their hesitancy. The oil they have likely been consuming is probably inedible or has no taste or has a thick, greasy consistency that would gross anyone out. But for me to be successful in teaching these basic techniques—tasting oil, swallowing a small amount, even enjoying some of it will all be required. I have attended events where I sampled fifty super high-quality, bitter EVOOs in one day, and at times, I felt woozy from all the polyphenols I had consumed. So a few sips won't harm you in any way.

I suggest sourcing one really superlative EVOO to use as a benchmark. Look in the reference section in your area for a specialty foods retailer or search online. The comparative sample will be either a bottle of oil already in your pantry or, if your curiosity is serious, purchase the smallest bottle of supermarket olive oil from one of the larger brands you recognize. You really don't need much for this tasting, but the remainder will not go to waste. If you aren't big users of EVOO yet, I suggest you look for an 8 oz/250ml bottle. Remember, the higher the price you pay, the more likely the quality will be what it is supposed to be. Hopefully, it retained much of its original excellence. You'll also need a few other items, which I'll list here:

- A glass or bottle of water
- A napkin
- An empty paper cup (preferred)
- A sliced green apple or unflavored cracker
- Wine glasses or small shot glasses from which to taste the oil

First, have all these items laid out. The green apple/crackers will help you diminish any "off tastes" or oiliness in your mouth. The water should be sipped between samples. The empty cup will be used to spit out any oil you don't deem worthy of swallowing. The napkin is to wipe your lips of any residual greasiness or spills.

Pour about two tablespoons of the two oils (the specialty and the older and/or lower-quality oil) into the two glasses. We will start with the expensive oil you purchased. It is always beneficial to taste a good oil before a bad one since the bad oil could alter your palate. Make sure not to mix them up. You can leave the bottles next to each sample for ease of identification. Put the glass in your hands, and cover the opening with your other palm. The goal here is to warm up the sample using your body temperature, trapping the aromas of the oil sample. Give that process a few minutes.

Once you feel the sample is ready, you'll start to smell it. Bring the glass close to your nose. Take slow, deep inhalations. We will go through our defects process of smelling the oil. As I detailed in Chapter Seven, if you can confirm an aroma of fruitiness from three inches away, meaning the glass opening is three inches from your nose or at your chin, that would be considered an "intense fruity" oil. If you must bring the glass opening to one inch from your nose, or just up to your nose, that sample would be classified as "medium fruity" or "medium intensity." And finally, if you need to place your nose all the way into the opening to ascertain an aroma, the sample would then be "mild," or "delicate."

All three are acceptable and varying cultivars produced differently by millers will result in any one of these three intensities. Which did you prefer? Did you enjoy the aromas of this new, more pricey oil? Did it help you fantasize about traveling to olive-oil-producing countries? Or did it remind you of superlative meals you've enjoyed where ultra-premium EVOO was served? I am not expecting you to be a professional taster like me. But extra virgin olive oil, by law, must have a fruity component greater than a median of zero. Meaning, the smell must convey some fruitiness. Olive fruit isn't fruity like a lemon. It is green fruity, like freshly cut grass, tomato leaf, almond, or herbaceous. Or it could be ripe fruity, like a ripe banana (not over-ripe or rotten), with a subtle, pleasant ripeness. If your purchase is reminiscent of either of these two fruity sensations, you are likely on your way to a good result.

Now, we need to taste the EVOO to confirm what our nose indicated to us. Because fruitiness is only one of the positive attributes you are seeking, it must also have some bitterness on your tongue and pepperiness (pungency) in your throat. But your sample must not have any defects present, or it legally cannot be labeled Extra Virgin. Remember the defects that we discussed at length in Chapter Seven? Go back to that list and confirm that you are not experiencing those smells. If so, I would urge you to continue the tasting anyway so you can grow in your knowledge of your oil purchases.

The next step is to prepare to taste the oil. We do not drink olive oil. And as we discussed, Americans have a reluctance to put oil in their mouths at all. But remember, every health practitioner worth their weight, recommends two servings of EVOO a day for optimal health benefits. A serving is a tablespoon, or 15 ml. So taking one taste straight is good for us, if, and only if, the oil is of high quality. You will allow a small sip of the oil to enter your mouth. But *don't* swallow it too soon. We need to chew on it. In layman's terms, this means to move the oil over our tongues. From side to side. Allowing any bitterness to register on our tongues. Your brain should be confirming the fruitiness you just smelled as well. Take the sip. Is it pleasant? Is there a nice bitterness in your mouth, perhaps like arugula?

Or is it flat? Does your mouth feel greasy? Do your lips feel greasy? Like if you had put on Carmex Chapstick? Is there any pungency? Or is it flat?

Again, at this point, if your mouth isn't happy, spit out the sample into the empty cup, take a well-deserved bite of the green apple or cracker and a generous sip of water and wipe your lips clean with the napkin. What did you think about this sample? Is it what you expected? Are you happy with that oil? Or perhaps you just had the "aha moment," where you realize that the EVOO world is complicated, and with a simple tasting session, you can establish that the oil you have been purchasing isn't really any good at all, and irrespective of how much you think you are saving, what you are doing is serving inadequate, likely mislabeled oil to you, your family, and your guests. And a change is needed.

Next comes the slurping. A very unsexy but necessary action to stimulate the pungency, a pepperiness, in the backs of our throats—referred to as retro-nasal. We keep the oil in our mouths and suck air through our clenched teeth, which aspirates or vaporizes some of the oil into a spray that hits the backs of our throats as we inhale. If the oil has a pungency, which, like bitterness, is a positive attribute, we should feel some stinging in the backs of our throats. It may tickle. It may make you cough. This is a good hurt. It's a signal that the oil is alive. Remember EVOO grade never receives heat during the manufacturing process, which is a typical kill step for bacteria in most shelf-stable foods. In essence, we are consuming a raw food product with no chemicals, heat, or pressure used to extract it from the paste. It is made by mechanical means only. If you are delighted with that small sample, I suggest you swallow it at this point. But if you really do not like straight oil, use your empty spit cup to discharge the remaining oil. You may feel a persistent bitterness and/or pungency. This is also a good sign.

When you try or use an EVOO that is green and peppery in the mouth and that gives you a subtle cough and has no defects, that oil is typically higher in antioxidants (compared to a lower-quality, volume brand you might see prominently displayed on shelves at your grocery store), which stem from the polyphenols present in exceptional EVOO. At the University of Pennsylvania, Dr. Gary Beauchamp studied the properties of high-quality EVOO to confirm a theory he had. The bitterness and pungency one might experience with these more expensive olive oils had a very similar chemical makeup to acetaminophen-oleocanthal. Phenols are known to provide health benefits. But the FDA is very strict, as I have written, about making health claims related to consuming olive oil.

To help decrease some of the bitterness in your mouth, you can take a bite of the green apple or cracker and a sip of the water to rid any flavor or residual oil from your mouth. Take a mental pause; did you like that oil? Is it surprisingly good? Better than you remember? Can you imagine it tossed on a salad? Or dipping bread into it?

To have a comparative experience, you need to taste the oil you had in your house before you begin to make your decision. You've now tasted a really great EVOO. It may or may not be too strong for you. That's your personal preference. Now, repeat the steps as we just did with the first sample with the suspected lower-quality oil. Don't be surprised if this next sample does *not* produce the fruitiness the previous one did. In fact, it may have no smell or have "off aromas." Remember this, even if nothing else sticks: If you experience any of these "off aromas," or any similar to them, the oil you have, if labeled "Extra Virgin," was either never good or is no longer good.

You can also do your tasting in a restaurant—albeit, modified. Ask the waiter for a large spoon. Usually, the oil is sitting on a table in a clear carafe with an open-pour spout. These are very clear signs that the oil will be defective. Likely rancid. Before using that oil on your food, smell it on the provided spoon first. Can you pick up any of those nasty aromas as warning signs? Take a small taste. Is it nasty in your mouth? There are two options here if the answer is yes to either your smell or taste test. One, ask the waiter if they have an unopened bottle he can bring to you and open it at the table. This will most certainly result in a strange look by the server. Second, avoid the oil and just eat without it.

The basics I have just shared are good first steps. If you have bad oil in your house, I suggest you discard it. If that isn't appealing, I would fry with it to use it up quickly. Remember, never pour oils down your drain. Just get rid of the container. I have been caught pouring bad oil into the backyard on my bushes.

In the next chapters, I will share ideas on how to use that bad oil you may have purchased recently and how to enjoy that great oil you will be bringing into your kitchens now. After you complete your home consumer tasting test, consider yourself deputized as an "at-home taster" by EVOOGuy.

Becoming a taster of olive oil is a long pursuit. After my first ONAOO class in Imperia, Italy in 2012, I connected with a group of five other English-speaking classmates from various countries, all equally as passionate and opinionated about olive oil as me. We ate many meals together that week and forged a brother and sisterhood of sorts and decided after many bottles of Prosecco and Limoncello, that we would get together, as a group, every harvest, in a different country to experience the bounty of the harvest together. To expand our knowledge, and along the way, perhaps we'd lend some assistance to the producers who we met and hosted us. We coined the name of the group: The Varietals (as in different varietals of olives).

There are over 900 varietals (cultivars) of olives that produce olive oil and many more times this in the actual derived products. So the education was open-ended. Our first visit was to Crete, Greece. What made it most memorable, aside from a lot of exposure to various production techniques and some amazing meals, was that I rented a private single-engine airplane with six seats, and as a private pilot, I flew our group—in two different flights—over the olive groves in Crete.

My group was thrilled, but to be honest, they were probably terrified too. The second year, we attended harvest in Italy. That was truly amazing. The places we saw, which most will never see because these are very private estates, changed me forever. My love affair with superior EVOO really bloomed on that trip.

In our third year, I organized—with some very experienced help—a week-long tour in Spain, the largest country for growing olives. Andalucía, Saville, and many more locales were on the itinerary. On this trip, we probably learned the most. We had a newspaper article writer follow us on many of our stops, and stories were written about our journey.

While the last trip with the Varietals was many years ago, I have very fond memories of many of those experiences and created some everlasting relationships with producers. My point is that it has taken me consistent dedication and high levels of education to know olive oil. I don't expect that of you, but what I have taught you in tasting is the best parts of what I know, all to protect you from olive oil fraud.

If you are a foodie like me, you are always thinking about what is next in the kitchen. Let's talk about all the wondrous ways you can use that great-smelling olive oil you have masterfully procured from the grocery store or online to cook and bake with in your kitchen.

EVOO FAST FACTS:

Extra virgin olive oil tasting is becoming very fashionable after decades of hesitation. The craft foods and beverages movements we see now, such as artisanal cheeses, beers, and chocolates, are opening the minds of curious consumers to learn how to taste and evaluate olive oil. Once you learn to smell and taste, you will be very comfortable with even testing the oil served to you at restaurants before you use it.

EVOO

CHAPTER ELEVEN
Your Kitchen, Your EVOO

You now have your beautiful new olive oil, tested by your smell and taste. You also perhaps have that rejected oil that you don't want to throw away and would like to cook with until it's gone. I will take you through the ins and outs of cooking, baking, and using both of these EVOOs in the kitchen, based on my culinary experiences in my own kitchen as well as the learnings from my global travels.

Many people prefer the essence a great EVOO imparts during the cooking process, yet there is a wide variety when it comes to the intensity of flavors. EVOO will lose some of its characteristics when used for cooking or baking (with heat), which is a natural change. And the flavor will be diminished.

Depending on the actual oil you chose, such as an intense culti-var or blend, there may be residual flavor remaining. I can assist you in pairing the olive oil for your palate with certain foods. For example, if you are someone who prefers a milder flavor, then make sure to use an oil that delivers a lower fruitiness. I will list some ideas on how to select an oil of various intensities in "Brands I Recommend" at the end of this book.

The number one question I am asked by olive oil consum-ers is "Can I cook with EVOO?" Many consumers have been greatly misled to believe myths, such as when olive oil gets hot, it is harmful. The answer is yes, not only can you cook with olive oil, but you must! Every cook and chef in Europe use EVOO for most of their dishes, and the majority in the US and Canada do as well. For many excellent restaurant chefs and celebrity chefs, EVOO is a critical part of their culinary tool chest. But, there are substantial differences in EVOO, as I have discussed in this book, and the first step must be that to be an EVOO chef in your own kitchen, you must verify that the oil you plan to use is acceptable, using the tasting guidelines I have laid out. You know what to do if isn't.

What does occur when you heat EVOO is that most of the health benefits will be "cooked off" in the heating process. You will want to cook up to 400°F, but again, the better the quality, the higher the polyphenols, the more stable the oil will remain when heated. Because quality EVOO is best known as an antioxidant, if you are cooking and heating the oil, it is being oxidized, there-fore negating its benefits for health. So I suggest not counting the oil that you cook with toward your two servings a day goal we talked about as recommended in Chapter Six. If indeed, you discovered through your initial tasting evaluation that you own a poor-quality olive oil, now is the time to use that sad oil to fry. I like to make chicken Milanese (easily find a recipe online) or bake lemony baby bliss potatoes with garlic. The high heat will burn off most of the unpleasant aromas or taste defects, and it will be hard to recognize in the foods you fry or bake in that oil.

My culinary education and enjoyment of foods cooked and fried in olive oil occurred in the extensive international travel I did with the olive oil industry. I have been privy to gourmet feasts made in rustic ways with superior EVOO and involved in every aspect of the meal. On a trip to Greece with my former brand, Gaea, I was taken to lunch at a roadside inn in the mountains of Crete just outside the port of Heraklion. A lovely older woman prepared traditional Cretan dishes for our arrival.

This meal was not unlike most of my Greek meals; however, it was outside, where a wood fire was built in the parking lot to prepare most of the food. She wasn't a professional chef but rather the innkeeper and knew how to cook well. The aromas from the area she was preparing our lunch were dream-worthy, and bottles of my Gaea EVOO were all over her cooking preparation table and on the outdoor dining table for us to add to our dishes. Yes, dishes had been prepared in advance, like the hummus, salads, dips, and spreads of all kinds, but the meat, a young lamb, was roasting over the wood embers. She brushed the lamb with EVOO every few minutes to keep it moist as the liquid fat dripped into the fire, causing it to flame up and kiss the meat with a subtle char. And I was told by our translator that she had marinated the lamb for hours in our EVOO with wild oregano, coarse salt, and garlic cloves. I couldn't wait to eat.

Greek woman frying potatoes in EVOO

Great EVOO is used daily in the Mediterranean diet by those who live in that region. The annual consumption of olive oil per capita is 24.7 liters per person in Greece, fourteen liters per capita in Italy, and nearly the same in Spain. In the US, it's less than 1 liter per person per year. That's the equivalent of two 17-oz bottles. And this includes food service. Very, very low. That's because most of us didn't grow up using it from childhood. Americans are still overly dependent on industrial-grade, refined, olive and vegetable oils, which have zero flavor or health benefits.

As great as the meal was that sunny fall day, and as full as we all were, the hosts had us on our feet dancing to traditional Greek guitar music. No dishes were broken, but it felt very *Mama Mia* to me. But we were warned that dessert was coming and to be ready to eat—again. I couldn't imagine after two hours of eating lunch, where we consumed all that spitfire-roasted lamb, *horta* (a traditional Cretan green found along the roads, boiled and then doused in EVOO), cheeses like fried halloumi, spreads, the bread we used to soak up the EVOO, and wine and Raki, the white lightning liquor drink of Greece, that we could handle another dish. But to my pleasant surprise, we were asked to watch our host prepare to drop donut batter into a black cauldron sitting over the fire, filled with local EVOO. We saw no smoke and smelled no "off" or greasy oil aromas. We perceived only fresh, green aromas emanating from that pot. And my guests and I were stunned that two gallons of EVOO were going to waste. Or were they?

We stared as she dropped spoonfuls of the batter into the very hot oil.

They fell below the surface and then sprung up to become visible again, with a hardening of the dough evident. It took only minutes in the near-boiling oil to fully cook the dough balls, called *loukoumades*, a Greek donut cooked in extra virgin olive

Greek woman frying Greek donuts in EVOO

oil. I had to try one right out of the oil, to see if they had a typical donut taste or if they were more savory due to the EVOO. They were not too sweet and there wasn't a strong olive oil flavor either. They certainly were not burned, as many think will happen if you fry in EVOO. And there was no smoking from the pot either. It was my first real "aha moment" when it came to cooking with EVOO. I had certainly been witness to many other variations in multiple countries, but never had I seen frying of this type. The *coup de grâce* was the thick, local Cretan honey that was poured over the *loukoumades,* and then each donut was stabbed with a toothpick for service.

Donuts drizzled with Cretan honey

The combination of the hot fried dough in EVOO and the gooey honey made this dish race up the chart of my top ten, best olive oil cooking finds—anywhere. My guests and I were finally beaten into a food coma that we wouldn't come out of for the rest of the day. Many of us passed on the planned dinner that night and chose to remember the meal that started and ended with EVOO.

So now you might be asking, "Okay, I am not in a rustic setting in Greece. I am in a townhouse in a metropolis. How can I make such delicious foods with my EVOO? I can't wait to answer that question because I, too, am an at-home cook, looking for simplicity, and since it is just the wife and me, low volume. I always recommend adding EVOO to at least one meal per meal period, providing you are at home where that oil is available. Think about how you like to eat, and add EVOO to the dishes or preparations as you can. Replace butter, margarine, canola, avocado, or coconut oils for the healthier fat of EVOO. Cook your eggs in it. Use it instead of salad dressing with a squeeze of lemon, or make a salad dressing with great EVOO and vinegar. Mix that vinaigrette for your sub sandwich. And if you like hummus, EVOO is often swimming on the top if you are eating out, but at home, you can do the same. Or drizzle it over a cooked steak instead of steak sauce.

Here is a simple EVOO break down into common meal periods:

Breakfast: Cook your eggs in EVOO, roast breakfast potatoes, fry sausage in a pan, use in pancake batter, or eat as they do in Spain: toasted rustic bread with a garlic clove rubbed on it, a slice of ripe tomato, a drizzle of great EVOO, and a pinch of salt. You replace EVOO with butter 1 to 1.

Lunch: Pour EVOO on a salad or greens in lieu of traditional salad dressing, which is typically loaded with sugar. Dress a sandwich with EVOO in lieu of mayo or sandwich sauce. Or make homemade mayo using the great EVOO.

Snack: Add EVOO to popcorn in lieu of melted butter. You'll be impressed.

Dinner: Any dish you sauté or roast and have used a low-quality olive oil or refined vegetable, nut, or seed oil, replace with great EVOO. It will elevate your meal. Oven-roasted veggies do particularly well when cooked with EVOO and a pinch of salt. The uses are endless—try your favorite go-to recipe, use your newly discovered EVOO, and see if you can tell the difference.

Dessert: EVOO drizzled over vanilla ice cream is decadent and luscious.

Vanilla ice cream with EVOO

In fact, there are a number of artisan brands that make chocolate with great EVOO. There are olive oil cakes that have been enjoyed for generations.

There are many fine books written about how to cook and utilize EVOO. I own a number of them. In fact, a few years ago I was asked to train the *Bon Appetite* editorial staff in their NYC offices about how to evaluate, taste, and handle EVOO.

In this hands-on session, I asked the staff why, when they write recipes, do they refer to EVOO as "olive oil" instead of "Extra Virgin Olive Oil," two very distinct products. When I shared regular olive oil (Pure and Light) with them, they were shocked at the difference in how their recipes tasted versus when they used Extra Virgin grade olive oil. Truth be told, they typically did use EVOO (including Lucini Italia). But they wrote the words "olive oil" in the recipe. The following November, the Thanksgiving issue came out, and it contained a seven-page article on EVOO, utilizing many of the takeaways I had shared with them. But in every recipe, they now used the words "Extra Virgin." Make sure you always use that grade in your culinary adventures. But verify that what you are preparing to cook with or consume is exactly as you wish it to be.

What you may not realize is that many foods you purchase already use EVOO as an ingredient. Good, quality jarred pasta sauces, salad dressings, some pesto, frozen meals, and even some cracker brands have exploited the EVOO craze and offer varieties of their products with olive oil, though mostly not EVOO grade. I generally don't pay much attention to these types of foods because you won't get your daily servings in a pre-packaged promise. You are much better off baking or cooking with a good EVOO.

For example, I don't use bottled salad dressing or marinades. I use a great EVOO I have, and if I need an acid, I will add red wine vinegar, real Balsamico di Modena IGP designation (not a fake with sugar and coloring added), or even lemon juice. With jarred pasta sauce, I look for a high-end brand I know, and then I add my own EVOO and usually some freshly crushed garlic and red pepper flakes to jazz it up. Once you become more accustomed to using EVOO in food preparation in the more popular ways we have spoken about—such as with rustic bread, on a green salad, with crudité, or drizzled over a Caprese salad or bruschetta—you can get creative in how you take in your two servings for health. Of course, I have met many people, particularly in Italy and Spain, who do a shot of EVOO straight in the morning. That really isn't going to be popular in America. But it should be. No wonder the average lifespan in the European Union is eighty-one as of 2020, and in the US, it is 78.9 years [EuroStat, 2021]. But in Italy and Spain, the average is eighty-three years. These are the two biggest producers of EVOO in the world.

Here are a few tricks to getting this wonderful and healthy fat into your diet:

In a smoothie: My wife has conditioned herself to add a tablespoon (1 daily serving = 15 ml) into her morning shake.

She believes this not only adds richness to the other ingredients but also improves the digestive challenges she is facing as she ages. And when combined with the other items, such as fresh and frozen berries, protein

Semone's daily smoothie with a pour of EVOO

powder, collagen, and water, the taste or bitterness of the EVOO is barely perceptible. Since she has been consuming high-quality EVOO the last eight years that we have been a couple, her annual blood work has improved—to the point that her doctor said she has the blood of a woman thirty years younger. She has become my biggest proselytizer.

To cook egg whites: I use two servings of EVOO to cook my egg whites. I like the eggs to almost fry in a lot of green, fresh EVOO. No matter what you add—or if you prefer to sauté some onions, other veggies, or even some meat in the pan before you add the eggs—great EVOO will impart some wonderful flavor. And it has no cholesterol, unlike the butter you are probably used to. We save great butter for our toast. That's about it.

On a baked potato: Lunch tends to be more challenging because many people either eat at work, away from the home, or have a sandwich. But on days off of work, or if you work from home, I recommend using EVOO for many lunch options. One of my favorites for lunch or dinner is a simple baked potato. In lieu of butter or sour cream, add 1–2 tablespoons of your EVOO of choice. Use a fork to stir the oil into the potato and smell the amazing aroma that this produces. Then add in some chopped scallions, or other favorite chopped veggie, with a pinch of Kosher salt. This makes a really hearty and warming treat. But these are starch and carbs, and the EVOO is good fat, so make sure you have a side of lean protein along with it to balance the meal.

On pizza: You can drizzle pizza with good EVOO.

But if you are dining out, your choices of an acceptable oil will be slim to none. So I suggest this: if you bring the pizza home or make one at home, drizzle it

Homemade deep dish pizza with Turkish organic EVOO

on when you eat it. Also, add it to your bowl of tomato soup or Gazpacho.

Drink it raw: I know this sounds hardcore, but when I have guests over for dinner, I make sure to consume at least one good serving of raw oil during our pre-meal noshing. That way, I'm both ensuring I'm getting my daily dose, and this helps fill me up so I will eat a smaller dinner. EVOO is satiating. It fulfills the need your brain has to be satisfied with a fat. So better to eat great olive oil with crudité than over-consume a heavy dinner that has far more calories and likely bad carbohydrates.

Anything starchy really elevates EVOO, which is why you keep seeing these kinds of foods aligned with olive oil. And when the starch is heated, that really expresses the aromas of great EVOO. Think pastas, potatoes, rice (risotto), breads, and pizzas. I have also suggested people prepare a Mediterranean dish with some canned tuna, white beans, baby tomatoes, some leafy greens, and maybe a piece of French bread and cheese. Drizzle the EVOO over all of these. This technique will enhance the flavor (and health benefits) greatly. But if you aren't able to consume EVOO during a lunch period, then dinner is going to have to be your go-to answer, especially if you weren't able to have your oil for breakfast either.

High heat and grilling: Cooking your dinner and incorporating EVOO is really very easy. Anytime I need to sear or sauté meat, veggies, or fish/shellfish, I use EVOO.

With a very high smoke point, upwards of 400°F (above frying), and a healthy fat, I always feel better about using EVOO to conduct heat and prevent sticking over any other oil, butter, Ghee, or fat alternative. If you are a big griller, marinating your meat in EVOO is essential.

Cooking shrimp in EVOO

Some people add soy sauce, garlic, acids like vinegar, or honey, but you must have oil as a base. Remember this oil is penetrating the fibers of the meat or fish you marinate in. So the better the quality of the oil, the better the resultant protein will be. Prior to grilling, I always brush or spray EVOO onto the grates to reduce sticking. Remember to verify the quality of the oil you are using even if it is a spray. Many national brands have EVOO spray, but that oil can have defects, which will make it unpleasant. Once you begin to grill, remember to baste the exposed sides with more EVOO to keep the meat or fish from drying out. Even then, when done, I usually give a healthy pour of EVOO over the finished food to add the flavor and moisture I desire, in lieu of a steak sauce, etc. The oil you drizzle on will be considered uncooked so it will retain many of the health benefits great EVOO delivers.

Favorite veggies: Nervous about having the future in-laws over or cooking dinner for that guy you have been dating? How about a business partner? Asparagus is a great side that I love to cook in good EVOO that looks a lot more sophisticated than it is. I learned in my early days to use a peeler to eliminate the woody exterior. But in reality, this is healthy fiber. So how do you tenderize it? I don't recommend steaming asparagus unless you really like it that way. Instead, take a sheet pan, line it with aluminum foil. Wash and dry your asparagus well and trim the lower 1–2" of the stalk. Preheat your oven to 375°F. Pour about two tablespoons of EVOO—I use more—onto the foil. Place onto the oil, a nice pinch of Kosher salt and freshly ground black pepper, and add the asparagus. Roll the spears so they are well coated by the oil. They must not overlap. Each stalk lays on its own in the oil. When the oven is ready, place the tray on a middle rack. Cook for approximately seven minutes, then check and shake the tray to move the stalks so the brown side is now facing up. Give it another seven minutes and check. If they look browned and have shrunk a bit, remove them and allow to cool. Serve immediately and you can even impress your guests with a discussion about the kind of olive oil you used and where it came from! They are wonderfully caramelized, tender, and have absorbed all the oil nicely.

This same process can be used for Brussel sprouts, another misunderstood vegetable, and also with green beans. Instead of using the oven, I par-boil my green beans, drain them, and then heat EVOO in a sauté pan, add shallots and small cherry tomatoes, then toss in the boiled green beans for a few minutes to coat them with the oil. Served hot, they are another crowd favorite. But if you truly wish to express the complexities of a great EVOO, steam or boil cauliflower flowerets to *al dente* and drain. Drizzle them immediately with the oil and use a dash of salt. The flavor of the oil shines through and even the squeamish who aren't fans of cauliflower will be converted for life.

Pasta: One of my all-time favorite meals I have made in the over fifteen years I have been in the olive oil business is a pasta dish. One hundred percent of the time when I make this, it's a winner. Rigatoni with Sausage and Greens. I actually have a hot version and a chilled version, better for summer. The hot meal starts with a real Italian-dried pasta cut called Mezze Rigatoni. I choose bronze cut, slow-dried pasta from Italy. Preheat your oven to 400°F. To finish the preparation, I secure a pound of hot Italian sausage links. A bunch of broccoli rabe (aka rapini), ends trimmed. I have my bottle of great EVOO handy, some dried red pepper flakes, four to six cloves of garlic, and some cherry tomatoes, which I halved. I chop the garlic. And in one large pasta cooker, I boil the water and salt it when rolling. I cook my entire box of pasta, al-dente, and follow the time on the box. Usually nine to eleven minutes. Drain. Toss with a small drizzle of EVOO to prevent sticking. Line a cookie sheet with aluminum foil. Drizzle some EVOO and place the sausage links on it. Poke the links with a paring knife to prevent bursting. I roll the links over the oil to ensure browning. I cook until they are brown and the juices are clear- about fifteen minutes. I let them cool. While the pasta water is still rolling, I add the rapini and cook quickly, removing them before they are too soft, and drain. I cut those into 2" pieces. In a large serving bowl I add my cooked pasta, season with salt and pepper, add the cut sausage pieces, the cooked broccoli rabe, the chopped garlic, the halved cherry tomatoes, a pinch of crushed red pepper flakes, and a glug of EVOO, about ¼–½ cup. Not too much, judge for yourself. Taste. If no other seasoning is needed, serve. This is a one-pot meal that almost everyone will be pleased with, and you'll also be consuming your days' worth of EVOO.

Chicken: My go-to, favorite chilled dish is called "Summertime Chicken Pasta." I pre-cook farfalle (bow tie) Italian pasta and coat it with EVOO to prevent sticking again. I pre-heat the oven to 375°F. I line a sheet pan with foil and drizzle EVOO all over it. I take boneless, skinless chicken breasts, wash and dry them, and set them on the oil in the sheet tray. Then, season with salt and pepper and cook until done, usually thirty minutes. I allow it to cool and then cut it into bite-sized pieces. I again have washed and halved cherry tomatoes. Some folks use sliced sun-dried tomatoes instead. Have about five to six chopped garlic cloves and the bottle of EVOO close by. I chiffonade fresh basil leaves and set aside. I assemble the cooked pasta, cut the chicken breast, and toss in the tomatoes and garlic. Add ¼–½ cup of EVOO, and season to taste with an emphasis on a bit more Kosher salt than usual—it will enhance the flavor. Toss in the basil and mix. Allow to chill for a few hours and serve. It's an amazing meal, and the leftovers are even better.

Baking: Cooking with EVOO also includes baking. I'm not much of a baker, I'll admit. I far prefer the free-form expression cooking with savory ingredients allows me. Baking is much more disciplined and requires exact measurements for the finished goods to come out of an oven successfully. Try making pizza dough from scratch, which is one baked item I do like to make. If you forget to use the right amount of yeast or water, the dough won't rise, and your crust will end up flat and hard. EVOO can be exchanged for melted butter in any recipe on a 1 for 1 scale, and you will be using a plant-based alternative with no cholesterol. Carrot cakes that typically use vegetable oil in their recipe (almost always refined, and who has ever eaten cottonseed?) can easily use EVOO instead. Pie crusts can also be made using EVOO, but the crust will need to be frozen first before filling. I have used EVOO in brownies I've made from scratch. There is a flavor component to be wary of. The fresher and more fruity the EVOO the more flavor it will impart. You can look for more mild EVOO that produces lower fruitiness. Oils that are made from Arbequina olives are one good choice. These usually originate from Spain, but California produces a lot of Arbequina oil. Nocellara del Belice, a southern Italian olive has been prized for being gentle and soft.

So you are ready to be an at-home chef with the top quality oils you bring into your house. With your smell and taste test, you can meet your expectation of quality. Then return what doesn't meet your palate. Remember, once a bottle is opened, the clock is ticking. Also, keep HALT in consideration. Many cooks and home entertainers like to leave a bottle of oil by the stove, as a reminder to grab it, and it's easy to do since it is close by to food prep areas. But that proximity to heat will ruin the oil very quickly—as quickly as with one good exposure to a hot cooktop, a pot of boiling water, or a hot oven.

Using EVOO throughout the day is not as complicated as one would think. I don't look at using a super-premium EVOO as lavish. It's a necessity. Watch any cooking show today on TV or streaming; the chefs and hosts almost unilaterally declare that good EVOO can make your dish better. And because of the higher fruitiness of premium EVOO, you use less of it for a greater impact. Of course, if you are eating away from your kitchen, you may be at the mercy of the olive oil available, unless you wish to bring your own. When I ran Lucini, Giada De Laurentiis, the well-known celebrity chef mentioned in a TV interview one day that she always carried with her our small Lucini Italia 1 oz EVOO travel packets to use with her out-of-home meals. She even pulled one out from her purse. If you are an olive oil enthusiast who feels compelled to always have great EVOO with you, there are little packets out there for purchase (see the Reference section). You may not want to carry a bottle, but I do suggest leaving a bottle at work to use on salads in lieu of bottled dressing, which often uses very low-quality oils, as well as many other ingredients, such as sugar and salt.

Food is beautiful.

How it is presented, created, and the ritual of its consumption.

We are also given the opportunity to make memories with our EVOO recipes with our families. Create a legacy and perhaps even find out your own history has some EVOO in the recipes of the past! Why go to all the work to present a lovely meal to your family, made of the freshest ingredients, and then skimp on the oil? Why serve an imposter EVOO?

Entertaining with EVOO

Every day that you, as a burgeoning consumer of quality EVOO, use and integrate better EVOO into your diet and meal planning, you are also ensuring that one of the best and healthiest foods, easily available to us, will become far more integrated into our lives. So do it now. And don't look back. Your pan is waiting for you.

EVOO FAST FACTS:

EVOO conversion with butter is a 1:1 ratio. Anywhere a recipe calls for 1 tbs of butter, replace with 1 tbs of quality EVOO. You may feel like you are missing the buttery flavor, but you are also losing the cholesterol and saturated fat.

CHAPTER TWELVE
Beat the EVOO Fatigue

Y ou are all fired up and inspired. Hopefully, you can't wait to be the best olive oil consumer ever. You are prepared to have your recommended two tablespoons a day for optimal benefits. People usually can keep this up for a few months, and then they are back to buying an easy bottle on the fly again. I understand that committing to better and more EVOO in your life needs to be a reframing of your lifestyle. All this change may seem exciting for a little while, and then the next thing you know, you are faltering and giving in to convenience-based olive oil again, due to a lack of time to shop for the best brands.

Knowing this, I invite you to learn my suggested ways to stave off what may be inevitable at some point in your new viewpoint of olive oil—EVOO fatigue. EVOO fatigue can appear as many types of malaise, just like with any other consumer fatigue we experience. The confusion most consumers feel when faced with a crowded olive oil section in a store, with shelves loaded with unusual brand names, multiple miss-messages on the labels, and varied pricing, is daunting. I witness this almost every time I walk by this section. I try to lend a hand to frustrated consumers when I can.

Another deflator of your enthusiasm may be all the hype in the news. Some of it is positive. But do the editors who are writing about olive oil really know the topic well enough to be reliable? Most of the news is fairly stressful, from bad olive harvests and "fake oils" to mafia-controlled distribution of some Italian oils and TV doctors offering seemingly misguided information. Sadly, the olive oil industry has had this polarizing moniker for hundreds of years, if not longer. In the modern time of food revolutions, where manufacturers are addressing multiple changes in eating needs, such as gluten-free, plant-based, Keto, and regenerative agriculture, the olive oil industry remains stoic in its antiquated positioning and offerings. No wonder we are all fed up hearing about olive oil!

Since smelling and tasting to identify quality EVOO is a new concept for you, let's say you ran, not walked, to your pantry and discarded any olive oil you had, realizing it was either not a good product, was perhaps mislabeled, or had just gone rancid. Much like with a diet, you one day decide, "It's time to lose this extra weight, and I'm making a change—today!" The same should be true with your olive oil. But also like most diets, it's hard to sustain. And you know by now, when I say "olive oil" I mean the real "Extra Virgin" grade. I ask myself, why do consumers give up on good EVOO? What will inspire them to take action and change again? Do you remember the day you finally admitted that you were being scammed by your olive oil brand? Embarrassed that you know food pretty well but olive oil was one of those items you just dismissed. Now, perhaps, if you have discovered a really great, authentic, well-cared-for bottle of EVOO, the simple joy of consuming a truly special product that meets your expectations is a big relief. One less challenge you need to be concerned with as you plan your meals and menus. And if you fall back to your old ways again of using just any old bottle that you found at a store or decanted from a stainless steel fusti at an "olive oil boutique" how will you feel then?

I have been exactly where you are now. I wasn't always concerned about the olive oil I purchased. It wasn't until I was in the olive oil industry that my eyes were opened. Before I began with Lucini Italia in 2006, I honestly cannot remember a brand name of EVOO I used. Probably, like many of you, whatever was on sale or on display at my local supermarket was what I grabbed. I'm not ashamed of this, nor should you be. As I've written, as Americans, good EVOO is not inherent to our diets like it is in Europe and around the Mediterranean. Olive oil is to them what ketchup is to us. Our national condiment. But ketchup is not nearly as good for us, usually containing a lot of sugar, artificial colors, and other food stabilizers.

Decide that today is the start of a new EVOO coming into your kitchen. You can even offer to show off your new tasting skills and share that experience with loved ones and friends. They will be impressed!

One hurdle you will face—once you convert—is the doubting Thomases. Be it immediate family members or friends. In the 1996 movie, *Mother*, starring Albert Brooks and Debbie Reynolds and terrifically funny even today, Albert Brooks is grocery shopping with his mother, played by Ms. Reynolds, and he selects a jar of the jam he loves off the shelf, which his mother perceives as expensive. She gives him a hard time about it, and he defends his choice with wit, by exclaiming that it is a simple luxury that makes him feel good. This earned him a snarky look. A similar scenario may play out for you—perhaps not at a grocery store but possibly in your kitchen when a family member sees a more elegant dark bottle of EVOO in the cupboard and inquires why you are switching to a "fancy brand." In reality, you aren't defending your decision, you are educating them, as I have done for you, that the bottle they purchased and tasted to verify its quality is real EVOO and will provide the taste and health benefits we all desire from good quality food. It elevates food and eating overall. In fact, isn't that why we eat? Primarily to nourish ourselves? Hearing objections is something I have grown used to. Unlike most executives in the olive oil business, I have spent my last few years as a self-employed entrepreneur, focusing 100 percent on olive oil education, consumer-facing tasting, and olive oil brand consulting, as well as developing and selling my own EVOO brand, which I will list for you in the last chapter.

As a consumer just like all of you, I often feel overwhelmed by choices in the market. Be they electronic, household, clothing, or, of course, food. Our culture is one of free enterprise—it rewards entrepreneurs who have developed products, brands, and companies that create items, which supposedly make our lives more complete. Or that's what they think or what their market research has told them.

Part of my olive oil journey at Lucini Italia involved extensive consumer marketing via qualitative research. The founders were very disciplined in learning before executing. And reducing the element of risk. This included even right-brained thinking, which a company based on this consumer marketing philosophy, conducted extensive research using hypnosis to try to establish from the paid participants why they make the purchasing decisions they do and what motivates them to select a brand of EVOO. This was a very expensive and time-consuming project prior to the company launching its brand. And this investment was one very good reason why I felt comfortable working for them. The results were journaled in a number of thick binders, which I read in their totality during my first months at the company. The ten-cents summary of all that research summed up said that consumers must be led to a product. They won't just discover it on their own. And they desire authenticity, to be reminded of a unique experience—perhaps one they had when traveling in countries like Italy or Spain. Steve Jobs, the founder of Apple, knew what the consumers wanted and needed (the iPhone) even before they did. And that they wanted to use only one finger to manipulate the screen. This is what made Apple so dominant in the cell phone industry when their original business was personal computing.

Lucini, I felt early on, had the ability to meet the consumers' needs, and my challenge became how to get the product into the right stores and promote it with limited funds, to gain consumer awareness and trial. The answer, in part, was influencers (celebrity chefs and notable media darlings like Oprah). Consumers trusted these people's recommendations. But this footprint of success isn't a fast one, isn't inexpensive, and requires deft management to execute the marketing strategy. Most olive oil brands do not have these skills inherent in their company DNA. So how will a consumer, like yourself, finally find the answers to their questions?

First, you must keep top of mind that your number one goal is to keep putting high-quality EVOO in your pantry. So it's time to just forget about any olive oil murmuring you hear. Just don't read about it, don't spend any more time thinking about it. My book will be the last endeavor you have to make prior to becoming your own "at-home taster." If you are an olive oil lover, then you have read or listened to hundreds of olive oil stories online, in magazines, or heard about this industry on TV. While there are sometimes some reliable sources of trustworthy information, unless you really can read between the lines, most of what is said about olive oil is just white noise or spin. We all know, or at least should, that much of the olive oil on most grocery store shelves isn't of good quality and likely doesn't meet the declaration of grade as listed on their label. And no amount of media will change this decades-old syndrome. Only the USDA/FDA can. Until then, you can only trust yourself.

Second, aside from what I have taught you about checking the country of origin or the "best before date," forget what the labels say. I have tried to be gentle but consistent about this. Labels are a marketing platform. There are FTC (Federal Trade Commission) and FDA regulations about what you can and cannot state on food packaging. Health claims about olive oil are very strictly narrow for a reason. So if you see claims offering healthier arteries and blood flow, better concentration, a boosted immune system, and many others, there is no allowable data that the FDA will allow any olive oil product to make these claims with. Further, images of peasants picking the fruit, artistic renderings of olive groves, and awards that may or may not be legitimate, all should be overlooked and no weight given to any of this when making a selection.

Third, don't be cheap. You will stay invested if you invest. If the price is too good to be true, it probably is. Remember every year olive oil producers have a new harvest that must be processed. That means oil that remains in their tanks months prior to the harvest must be emptied to make room. Therefore, bottles are filled and shipped to US warehouses and the sales teams are pressured to dump the bottles at reduced prices to create the sales necessary to move a lot of this excess inventory. So in the Northern Hemisphere, where the biggest producers are—Spain, Italy, Greece, Tunisia, Turkey, and Portugal—their harvest is October through January. Sometimes later if their quality is really low. So look for hot deals around the holidays. Sometimes these prices are attractive on better quality brands and you should take advantage of them. But more likely, you will see lower quality oils really push hard to move a lot of volume, and then you may be tempted to buy more of this very low-quality oil. But be strong. Remember, you should know the brand well before you commit to a larger purchase.

Lastly, becoming the "at-home taster" as I have recommended in this book is a must. You will forever be taken advantage of and continue using low-quality, perhaps mislabeled EVOO if you aren't prepared to judge the contents of every bottle of olive oil you buy and just blindly trust the producer/brand. Do you test drive a car before you buy it? Do you watch a trailer of a movie before you pay to see the entire film? And do you look at the condition of the meat and produce you purchase at the store before you buy it? Of course. And now, you smell and taste the olive oil you buy. Every time. And at every restaurant.

Over the years, I have become a very distrusting consumer. Working in this industry that is rife with challenges and false claims, as well as consumer fatigue over this product specifically, has jaded me. In fact, at many Olive Oil 101 classes I have taught with actual consumers, not just the trade, I ask them to bring a bottle of the olive oil they are using now from home so we can evaluate it together.

A tasting class for neighbors

In one situation, a family came in with a bottle with no brand label, but a clear bottle, a cruet, with an open pourer, and an orange-looking substance inside. I introduced myself and welcomed them to the class. Once they were seated, I thanked them for bringing the sample, and before I walked away, I asked them to remember these words, "That oil is disgusting and you will agree with me before this class is over." The faces on these people, but specifically the husband, were priceless. You would have thought I insulted a family member. In reply to my exaltation, the father said, "How can you know that? You haven't even tried it," and disagreed with me in defense. I didn't answer him, and I smiled and walked away to greet the others.

After the sixty minutes of discussion and presentation, I guided the class through a tasting of nine oils. Varying from good to bad, poor to average, better to inedible, to really good, ending in fantastic! This back and forth process allowed them to calibrate their skills of smell and taste, and with my assistance, they learned what a real EVOO should taste like, and what some defects, which would make an olive oil not acceptable as an EVOO grade, also tasted like. And during this class, I kept my eye on this family with the orange sample. I could see change was happening. At the end of the planned tasting, I went around the room and I tasted oils that people had brought in to me for evaluation. Some of them were store brands. Others were oils they had dragged back from overseas trips. Or a bottle they discovered at high-end stores like Sur la Table. Each time I was able to help them discover the truth about the bottles. The sad truth. And when I ended up with the family who I warned had a terrible bottle of oil, the husband volunteered that their oil was rancid, and compared to fresh, healthy real EVOO, theirs was inedible. They were embarrassed and acknowledged that indeed

I was right, just from the visual inspection I made. I left this group with the same message I leave all my attendees: quality EVOO isn't a choice; it's a must. Anything less and you are cheating yourselves, your family, and your guests.

Change is hard. It is meant to be. But once you are conditioned to it, you will be a much better consumer of real EVOO. And you will share this newfound interest with friends and family, and hopefully, they will trust you and make changes in their homes as well. Or share this book or encourage them to buy one and then pass along the newfound skills to their connections. If we all make a small change in our diet by only purchasing and consuming quality, properly labeled, fresh-tasting extra virgin olive oil, and never giving prey to the low priced supermarket products we have all purchased in the past, the industry will respond with brands elevating their product to meet the changing and growing demands of the buying public. Just like organic foods were a fringe industry before the USDA regulated them in October 2002 with the National Organic Program, they have become a $50 billion annual business in the US alone. Every grocery store in America has and promotes organic foods. And the labels are consistent about that claim. One day olive oil will be similarly successful in its appeal to the American public. But only with you, the consumer, adopting quality and change will it move in that direction. And then the fatigue we all feel will dissipate.

EVOO FAST FACTS:

There are currently over 1000 different bottles of olive oil sold in US food stores. This doesn't account for e-commerce assortment. This is far too many without the proper oversight. As this book has illuminated, many of them claim to be extra virgin grade and likely are not. So it is very easy for any consumer to feel overwhelmed at the point of sale. Just use the tips you have learned and look past all the hype, displays, and low prices, to find a true bottle of EVOO.

Conclusion

The Journey Forward

We started our journey together with some simple and frequently asked questions. You now have all the answers, and the time has come for you to go out and proactively buy and consume that oil. Choose not to skimp and save on one of the biggest consumable areas of your kitchen.

I don't want you to feel any shock that you have been purchasing olive oil without the benefits of expertise or a proper explanation about how to make wise decisions. You know what to do with the bad oil in your pantry, and you know that you can start cooking with the good oil, so let's get busy. We cannot be experts on everything or rely on instincts or be swayed by family history or even store promotions to drive our decision-making.

My commitment to this industry is to continually learn and adapt to the changes this product presents. This is all geared to supporting you, the consumer. I have provided the information you need to avoid the pitfalls and being taken advantage of by so many of the brands that you are used to buying. When I say that I want to talk to anyone and everyone who has questions, big or small, about olive oil, I am not kidding. Here is my email address: david@evooguy.com. I will email you back personally or you can also look at some of the blog posts or social media posts I put on my website, www.evooguy.com.

I also know that even if you read this book, you may still be skeptical, so I want to be transparent with my information. You may also be beyond curious and want to delve even more into some of the organizations that support olive oil. On my website, I list many relevant websites, such as for the USDA and other olive oil resources, so you can stay updated and informed. They obviously may change from time to time, but I have not seen the needle move a lot in oversight and governance—another reason why it is so important for you to know how to taste your own oil.

When you decided to read (or listen) to this book, you made a proactive commitment to expanding your knowledge and facilitating change. I feel certain that by now, you will have accomplished the former and are prepared for the latter. It is now time for you to pay it forward by sharing your newfound knowledge. Encourage your friends, family, and colleagues to buy this book. Or give them yours. But more than that, invite them over to taste your newly discovered EVOOs. And demonstrate your tasting skills. They will be impressed and thankful. You have now been knighted as an "at-home taster."

In the next section, I provide you with the resources that I have found useful in understanding the complicated world of olive oil. It's a very wide range of noted authorities, most of whom I know and some I know very well. Take the information at face value.

Resources You Will Need as an At-Home Taster

(as of late 2021)

Note: Read the information but always use your palate as the final judge.

Regulatory
USDA
International Olive Council (IOC)

Trade & Educational Associations:
Mediterranean Diet Roundtable
North American Olive Oil Association
California Olive Oil Commission
QV Extra (quality seal)
Extra Virgin Alliance (quality seal)
Slow Food USA
AOCS

UC Davis Olive Center
ONAOO (Olive Oil School)
Women in Olive Oil
Oldways (Cultural Food Traditions)

Guide Books/Recognition:
Flos Olei (Guidebook)
EVOOLEUM (Guidebook)

Editorial/News:
Olive Oil Times (e-publication)
OliMerca: (Spanish language e-news)
Mercacei: (Spanish language e-news)
OHIS (Olive Health Information System)

Medical & Academic Professionals:
Dr. Andrew Weil
Dr. David Katz
Dr. Simon Poole
Mary Flynn, PhD
Dr. Gary Beauchamp (Oleocanthal Society)
Dr. Artemis Morris
Sue Langstaff (Applied Sensory LLC)
Dr. Orlando Gonzalez

Notable Stalwarts:

USA
David Neuman, EVOOGuy: www.evooguy.com

Dean Karnazas: ultramarathoner
Alexandra Kicenic Devarenne
Liz Tagami
Daniele Santini
Chef Maria Loi
Daniella Puglielli
Maria Reyes
Joseph Profaci

Italy
Tom Mueller, Author, *Extra Virginity*
Marcello Scoccia
Carlotta Pasetto
Marco Oreggia
Lucio Carli

Spain
Santiago Botas
Agustí J. Romero Aroca
Rosa and Paco Vano
Jose Antonio Peche Marin Lazaro
Gerard Jara
Javier Sanchez Pedros
Alexis Kerner

Greece
Eirini Koklaki
Lisa Radinovsky

Brazil
Chania Chagas
Marcelo Scofano

Switzerland
Silvan Braun
Antonella Meyer-Masciulli

France
Emilie Borel Berta
Emmanuelle Dechelette

Holland
Francesca de Ritis

Canada
Fil Bucchino

Australia
Paul Miller

South Africa
Nick and Brenda Wilkinson

Japan
Toshiya Tada

Brands I Recommend

Links to these producers can be found on my website, www.evooguy.com.

Let me make this very clear, not one of these brands has paid me or asked me for inclusion in this book. I simply believe they represent the kind of high-quality EVOO I hope you endeavor to buy. I also give all the reasons why I think the oil is right and that way, should they ever not sell their oil anymore, you can take their qualification and qualities and measure it up against another producer. You can also email me and ask. Then if you are not happy with what you find, remember the process: you take the oil home and taste it like you should with every oil, and if it has clearly been on the shelf too long, you return it. If what you want is not available, here are some of my favorite online sellers who do a decent job with shipping and having fresh harvest oils. You should only be purchasing single-country-of-origin EVOO to reduce the chance of defects from blending.

Note 1: I will not suggest any Mediterranean or multi-country blended oils as these can be the most problematic with quality issues. But some of the brands I do recommend produce those oils. I recommend you avoid them.

Note 2: The brands listed are available to a greater or lesser degree in the US. There are many brands I love that are not available as of this writing in the US, so I have left them off—but they are not forgotten by me.

Spanish EVOO

EVOOGuy.com—Semone Extra Virgin Olive Oil, 500 ml and 100ml. 100 percent single-estate Spanish, from the region of Andalucía in Jaen. A Piqual mono-cultivar, with only green olives, hand-harvested early in the season, and the oil is maintained under nitrogen from storage to the bottle. Sold online on my website and at select events (pre-COVID). Produced by the famed Castillo de Canena. $30 a bottle for one 500ml, $9 for the 100ml. Discounted for multiple bottles. See www.evooguytruck.com.

Castillo de Canena—Arguably the #1, top-rated EVOO brand in the world. Flow Olei Guide #1 for 2020 and 2021 with a score of 100/100. Mario Solinas winner. From a remarkable brother and sister team, Francisco and Rosa Vano, of Jaen Spain. 100 percent Spanish. 100 percent single-estate grown, crushed, stored, and bottled. The care, effort, and money they have invested in carrying on their family tradition speaks to you in every bottle. I have been to their estate, stayed at their castle, and dined with them all over the world. Truly remarkable people. Many types of products, including biodynamic, which is rare. Found in better stores and online. Prices range but expect to pay upwards of $28-plus per 17 oz bottle, less for the 8 oz.

Casas de Hualdo—Another highly-decorated brand from Spain. Flos Olei 98/100 in 2021 and in the top five of all brands reviewed. Single-estate, located near Toledo, which is a short drive from Madrid. I have been fortunate to stay with them and learn how they create their magic during harvest. They produce many of the popular cultivars and bottle most of them as mono-cultivars, except a few items like their Riserva. They have a secondary line called Rockin Olive, which is lower-priced for a more mature olive used to make the oil. They also produce a child's EVOO, which is unique and clever. Their pricing can range from $10 for the 8 oz to over $20 for the 17 oz. Available in better stores and on their website.

Valderamma—This brand is produced on two estates owned by Miguel Millan, one in Toledo Spain, and one in Cordoba. I spent a few days with Miguel walking both estates and in both of his mills during harvest. Their attention to detail is a claim to fame. Their focus is mostly on foodservice, restaurants, and chefs. Therefore, the oils have been matured more than other similar, excellent EVOOs in their region to moderate the bitterness and pungency that can sometimes overshadow dishes. They are sold in fine food stores in the US, and their prices range, but expect to pay $20 for a 17 oz bottle. They produce a lot of organic oil, in particular a unique cultivar known as Ocal.

Mis Raices—which means "our roots." Victor Moreno Pastor and his cousin Carlos Pastor, 100 percent Spanish and from the northern region of Aragon, on family land in Orliete. A multi-generational estate growing the ripe Empeltre olive. Their oils are delicate in flavor. I have visited a few times both during harvest. These huge trees take hours to harvest by hand and yield only five liters of oil. Priced around $18 for their 500 ml bottles, found in better retailers. Learn more about them on their website.

Alcala Olivia—from Jaen, Spain, produces these amazing mini, single servings of quality EVOO (both organic and non-organic) called MiniOliva(R). They range in sizes from 8 ml to 14 ml and are sold in olive-shaped containers. They produce true EVOO as well as infused olive oil, vinegars, and dressings. They are new to the US but expanding. They are a family business that, for twenty-plus years, has been envisioning a way to deliver quality, convenience, and value in one dose. Santiago Perez Anguita and his daughter Angela Perez Linde and his family work hard to meet the growing needs of consumers around the world who realize that an open bottle of olive oil has a finite amount of time before it turns rancid. Look for these online and in better locations.

Italian EVOO

Entemio by Daniele Santini—100 percent Italian, available on his website. Typically $28 for a 250 ml bottle. Daniele visits the groves in Italy many times a year so sources the best farms, producers, and oils he can for the new harvest. He pays for their best quality and packages his bottles with Argon to protect the quality. He is a professional taster like me and, as such, has a very well-trained palate.

Frantoio Franci—When I write his name, I would associate his level of excellence to any Michelin chef, master wine vintner, and even a car manufacturer like Ferrari. Giorgio Franci built his business learning from his father in Montenero d'Orcia in the Grossetto region of Tuscany. His mill, which I have visited many times, sits high above his groves in an almost impossible location for large production. But they have been making the world's best EVOO for decades. Their attention to detail is unmatched. They are also a Flos Olei Hall-of-Fame producer and have been number one many years. If you find their oil, buy it. No matter the price. It's hard to find in stores, but Eataly features them. Expect to pay over $50 for a 17 oz bottle.

Monini—Today, Zeferino Monini oversees an empire that was started one hundred years ago by his grandfather, Zeferino Monini. They have risen to become the number-one-selling brand of EVOO in Italy. Based in Spoleto, Umbria, I have been fortunate to meet Mr. Monini at their plant and was rightfully intimidated by his accomplishments. Since 2000, they have been selling in the US under the watchful gaze of Marco Petrini. They have a wide range of products, but I am a big fan of their newer and more limited organic mono-cultivar EVOOs, which include Coratina, Frantoio, and Nocellara. What some don't know is that while two of these olives originate far south of Umbria, Monini trucks the olives on their day of harvest to their mills in Spoleto to crush them rather than purchasing the oil and bottling it with nitrogen. They have products best-suited for everyday use that can sell for $13 for a 17 oz bottle, up to their organic oils that can be as high as $25 for the same size. They can be found in many popular stores and online.

Bonolio—Salvatore Russo-Tiesi runs the US division of this Sicilian brand of excellent EVOO. Beautifully packaged, these oils are more delicate in intensity due to the warmer climate of their region. Most of their products carry a distinguished PGI designation, which means their olives are grown in a protected area, and they only use fruit from that region. While some of their products are blends from various countries, I recommend sticking with their 100 percent Italian oils. Their products are widely sold in stores and online through Amazon. Pricing runs $18 for a 17 oz PGI Sicily EVOO. Great people, great product.

Gonelli 1585—This family business and their jaw-dropping estate sit above Florence in a small village called Reggello in Tuscany. They have been growing olives for extra virgin olive oil and making fantastic products since 1585 on this estate, called Santa Tea. The original mill remains on their property where the foundation stone is engraved with the placement date. Today their oils rival most of the top brands produced in Tuscany by artisanal millers. But they have a large-scale operation. The youngest son, Giorgio, runs the business now, and I have been fortunate to do business with him for over a decade. Their oils are in the US but not prominent. If you can find them, expect to pay over $25 for a 17 oz.

Olio Mimi—A very small producer in southern Italy, Donato Conserva is a darling of the quality EVOO producers in Italy. He is a top-rated Flos Olei brand and his limited production of a few popular cultivars, such as Coratina (super intense) and Ogliorola (medium intense), are simply divine. I am conflicted to list them because they aren't easily found in the US. I sold them last year on my website. But they are really one of my favorite oils, so it's worth it for me to list them here and hope they will become available again. I sold their small bottles (8 oz) on my website for $20.

IL Vulcino—An amazing discovery. A wonder. An ancient extra virgin olive oil made with love by a wonderful couple living in a small village 100 km from Rome. Eugenie Grigolini is the face of the brand and a delight. The cultivars are Frantoio, Leccino, and an Etruscan olive called Caninese. Think of a blend of local olives as an orchestra. Each instrument works in harmony, and together, they form a sound where the sum is greater than each individual. And each year the harvest delivers a varied product that is a result of fantastic weather, the superb care of the trees, and the skill of the miller. This product is organically grown. It is the goal of Eugenie to play classical music via speakers from her archives to the trees to encourage and support their wellbeing. The flavors are abundantly fragrant, herb-like, and very central Italian, with a corresponding intensity of bitter and pungent finish.

Abandoned Grove—Fil Bucchino spends months every year scouring Italy, his homeland, to seek out the best trees he can that meet his expectations to produce the best

EVOO he can. At Abandoned Grove, they produce limited quantities of premium early harvest extra virgin olive oils, derived from groves that, once abandoned, have been restored to their former glory. The oil must be pre-ordered before harvest. They are based in Toronto, Canada.

Turkish EVOO

Oleamea—Merve and Patrick Doran make this 100 percent Turkish oil. It's organic (as of this writing). They are a young couple based in Boston with a family heritage of olive oil and quality. Their two bestselling mono-cultivars retail for $18 to $20 for 17 oz (500 ml). They also produce a unique two-pack gift set and food-service tins. They work only with their farms and local farmers in their area who meet their standards. Their oils are all bottled with nitrogen to protect quality. You can find them in better stores and on their website.

USA EVOO

McAvoy Ranch—This sophisticated EVOO was the brainchild of Nan McAvoy decades ago. She imported Italian olive trees, such as Frantoio, and cultivated them into a respectable business in northern California, to be purchased mostly through mail order. They are sold in their own shops and in limited retailers. Expect to pay $35 for a 375 ml bottle. But this is a stellar example of how to grow, crush, and bottle exceptional oil.

43 Ranch—A smaller producer in California, but their oils are divine. Their attention to quality is unmistakable. They are humble in their approach to the business and their packaging and very family-centric in their branding. I keep some of their oil in my cupboards as fruity examples. Their Helen's Blend is my favorite. It sells out quickly. $32 for 17 oz.

South African EVOO

Rio Largo—Brenda and Nick Wilkinson created this lovely brand on an estate they purchased in South Africa as a post-retirement business. They planted cultivars unique to the region and produce amazing EVOOs. Given they are in the Southern Hemisphere, I count on these as my fresh oil supply in our summertime. They bottle their oils both in traditional glass as well as bag-in-box tubes, which really is the best way to package quality EVOO: no light, no air, and with a vacuum to allow only oil to decant while preventing air from flowing back into the package. Not easily available, but check their website for options. Pricing is hard to quote.

Cypriot (Cyprus) EVOO

Atsas—I just ran into this oil, and they sent me some samples to evaluate. It's organic, and the producers explained to me this product is one of the "highest polyphenolic" olive oils bottled anywhere. I cannot verify this, and the FDA will not support most health claims. That said, it has a great taste and is well-packaged. It is not available in US stores as of this writing, but you can try to find it online.

Greek EVOO

Terra Creta—Based in Chania, Crete, they are one of the larger producers of quality EVOO in Greece, certainly on the Island of Crete. I visited in 2012, shortly after their facility expansion. I can say that since then, their oils have vastly improved—so much so that they won the coveted Mario Solinas Award in 2021, first place for "Ripe Fruity." They worked with Marco Scano, likely the leading blender to create the best EVOOs available. There are limited US sales, but I expect them to grow, and they can be found on Amazon for around $18 for a 500 ml.

Lonely Olive Tree Organics—A product produced by a Greek-American chef and restaurateur, Dimitri Kallianis. This sole EVOO is produced from his family's land and a surrounding area in Spare, Greece using PDO olive varieties. This oil, while typical of Greece, meets a higher standard and is revered by restaurants and retailers all over the US. His oils are sold in various sizes that make it easy to choose what's best for your family.

Loi Ladi Extra Virgin Olive Oil—A favorite, especially in New York City, where its creator, celebrity chef Maria Loi, is based and her restaurant thrives. Her one-liter is available in many stores and has also been sold on QVC. It's a 100 percent, Cretan EVOO, and the producer is well-known and respected for high quality. A medium fruity, you can't go wrong using this oil for many of your dishes where a cup of EVOO is needed.

How to Find Great Oils

Retail Stores by Region:

Northwest: Costco (all), Zupan's, World Foods, Metropolitan Markets, Delaurtentis, New Seasons Markets

West Coast: (So Cal) Bristol Farms, Vons/Pavillions, Lassens, Mothers, Erewhon

West Coast (Nor Cal): Rainbow Grocery, Lunardi's, Nugget, Molly Stone's, Zanotto's, World Market (all)

Rocky Mountains: Sprouts (all)

Southwest: Central Markets, AJ's, Whole Foods (all)

Midwest: City Olive, Fresh Thyme, Eataly, Mariano's

Northeast: Murray's Cheese, Fairway, Wegman's, Kings/ Balducci's, DiBruno Bros., Eataly, Roache Brothers

Mid-Atlantic: Harris Teeter, De Cicco's, MOM's

Southeast: The Fresh Market (all), Rouses Markets, Lowes

E-Commerce: (not brand specific)

EVOOGUYTRUCK.com

OliveoilLovers

Zingermans

Amazon

Olive Oil Tools of the Trade:

Argon Gas to add to an open bottle of EVOO for preservation

Defects Wheel: learn the defects that ruin EVOO

The quote I suggest you live by now after finishing my first book on EVOO is:

Know the Oil You Use & Use It Liberally

—David, a.k.a. EVOOGuy

About the Author

Credit to Little Photography

D avid M. Neuman began his olive oil career as a commis chef at the Four Seasons Hotel, Washington, D.C., in 1985, cooking with great olive oil. After years of employment in the specialty and natural foods industry, he was hired as president and partner of Lucini Italia, and for the next nine years, grew it to become the premier Italian olive oil brand in America. Upon selling the business in late 2014, David opened Gaea

North America with the assistance of its parent company, Gaea Products S.A. in Greece. In mid-2018, David continued his passion for EVOO by founding EVOOGuy.com®, a consultancy focused 100 percent on best-in-class extra virgin olive oils. At the same time David was launching his own EVOO brand, he was establishing a tasting tour using a custom-designed olive oil truck, lecturing, and continuing to share his knowledge via his Olive Oil 101 platform. David and his wife currently reside in Bluffton, South Carolina.

A free ebook edition is available with the purchase of this book.

To claim your free ebook edition:

1. Visit MorganJamesBOGO.com
2. Sign your name CLEARLY in the space
3. Complete the form and submit a photo of the entire copyright page
4. You or your friend can download the ebook to your preferred device

Morgan James
BOGO™

A **FREE** ebook edition is available for you
or a friend with the purchase of this print book.

CLEARLY SIGN YOUR NAME ABOVE

Instructions to claim your free ebook edition:
1. Visit MorganJamesBOGO.com
2. Sign your name CLEARLY in the space above
3. Complete the form and submit a photo of this entire page
4. You or your friend can download the ebook to your preferred device

Print & Digital Together Forever.

Snap a photo

Free ebook

Read anywhere